my revision notes

Edexcel AS/A-level History

RUSSIA, 1917–91:
from Lenin to Yeltsin

Robin Bunce

HODDER EDUCATION
AN HACHETTE UK COMPANY

Every effort has been made to trace all copyright holders, but if any have been inadvertently overlooked, the Publishers will be pleased to make the necessary arrangements at the first opportunity.

Although every effort has been made to ensure that website addresses are correct at time of going to press, Hodder Education cannot be held responsible for the content of any website mentioned in this book. It is sometimes possible to find a relocated web page by typing in the address of the home page for a website in the URL window of your browser.

Hachette UK's policy is to use papers that are natural, renewable and recyclable products and made from wood grown in sustainable forests. The logging and manufacturing processes are expected to conform to the environmental regulations of the country of origin.

Orders: please contact Bookpoint Ltd, 130 Milton Park, Abingdon, Oxon OX14 4SE. Telephone: +44 (0)1235 827720. Fax: +44 (0)1235 400454. Email education@bookpoint.co.uk Lines are open from 9 a.m. to 5 p.m., Monday to Saturday, with a 24-hour message answering service. You can also order through our website: www.hoddereducation.co.uk

ISBN: 978 1 4718 7637 0

© Robin Bunce 2017

First published in 2017 by
Hodder Education,
An Hachette UK Company
Carmelite House
50 Victoria Embankment
London EC4Y 0DZ
www.hoddereducation.co.uk

Impression number 10 9 8 7 6 5 4 3

Year   2020   2019 2018

Cover photo © Galina - Fotolia
Illustrations by Integra
Typeset by Integra Software Services Pvt. Ltd., Pondicherry, India
Printed in Spain

A catalogue record for this title is available from the British Library.

My revision planner

REVISED

Key Topic 5: Historical interpretations: What explains the fall of the USSR, c.1985–91?

Introduction

About Paper 1

Paper 1 Option Russia 1917–91: from Lenin to Yeltsin requires a breadth of knowledge of a historical period, as well as a knowledge of the historical debate around the fall of the Soviet Union. Paper 1 tests you against two Assessment Objectives: AO1 and AO3. AO3 is a new objective for this specification.

AO1 tests your ability to:
- organise and communicate your own knowledge
- analyse and evaluate key features of the past
- make supported judgements
- deal with concepts of cause, consequence, change, continuity, similarity, difference and significance.

On Paper 1, AO1 tasks require you to write essays from your own knowledge.

AO3 tests your ability to:
- analyse and evaluate interpretations of the past
- explore interpretations of the past in the context of historical debate.

On Paper 1, the AO3 task requires you to write an essay which analyses the work of historians.

At A Level, Paper 1 is worth 30 per cent of your qualification. At AS Level Paper 1 is worth 60 per cent of your qualification. Significantly, your AS grade does not count towards your overall A Level grade. Therefore, you will have to take this paper at A Level in order to get the A Level qualification.

Structure

At AS and A Level, Paper 1 is structured around four themes and one historical interpretation.

The exam is divided into three sections, which relate to different aspects of your course:

Aspect of the course	AO	Exam
Theme 1: Communist government in the USSR, 1917–85	AO1	Section A and Section B
Theme 2: Industrial and agricultural change, 1917–85		
Theme 3: Control of the people, 1917–85		
Theme 4: Social developments, 1917–85		
Historical interpretations: What explains the fall of the USSR, c.1985–91	AO3	Section C

The exam

The Paper 1 AS exam and A Level exam both last for 2 hours and 15 minutes, and are divided into three sections.

Section A and Section B test the breadth of your historical knowledge of the four themes:
- Section A requires you to write one essay from a choice of two. Section A questions will usually test your knowledge of at least a decade. You should spend around 35 to 40 minutes on Section A; this includes making a brief plan.
- Section B requires you to write one essay from a choice of two. Section B essays usually tests your knowledge of a third of the period 1918–79, around 23 years. You should spend around 35 to 40 minutes on Section B; this includes making a brief plan.

Section C tests your knowledge of the debate around the fall of the USSR.
- Section C requires you to answer one compulsory question relating to two extracts from the work of historians. Questions will focus on the years c1985–91. You should spend around 35 to 40 minutes on Section C, and an additional 20 minutes to read the extracts and make a plan.

The AS questions are of a lower level in order to differentiate them from the A Level questions. You will find examples of AS and A Level questions throughout the book.

How to use this book

This book has been designed to help you to develop the knowledge and skills necessary to succeed in this exam. The book is divided into five sections – one for each of the four Themes in depth, and one for the Historical interpretation. Each section is made up of a series of topics organised into double page spreads. On the left-hand page, you will find a summary of the key content you need to learn. Words in bold in the key content are defined in the glossary. On the right-hand page, you will find exam-focused activities. Together, these two strands of the book will take you through the knowledge and skills essential for exam success.

There are three levels of exam-focused activities.
- Band 1 activities are designed to develop the foundational skills needed to pass the exam. These have a green heading and this symbol:
- Band 2 activities are designed to build on the skills developed in Band 1 activities and to help you achieve a C grade. These have an orange heading and this symbol:
- Band 3 activities are designed to enable you to access the highest grades. These have a purple heading and this symbol:

Each section ends with an exam-style question and model high-level answer with commentary. This should give you guidance on what is required to achieve the top grades.

Establishing Communist Party control, 1917–24

Russia experienced two revolutions in 1917. The first, the February Revolution, led to the downfall of the **Tsar**. The second, the **October Revolution**, led to the creation of a radical new Communist government led by Lenin.

The creation of a one-party state

Lenin and the Communists promised a radical democratic government in which workers, soldiers and peasants governed themselves through **soviets**. However, by 1922 Lenin had created a Communist dictatorship of a one-party state.

Lenin's ideology

Lenin seized power because he wanted to replace **capitalism** with **socialism**: a new social system that would allow all people to be genuinely free and equal. Lenin was a Marxist and following the German philosopher Karl Marx, he believed that history progressed through a series of stages. This had important implications for Russia as the Russian economy was only beginning to industrialise, and Lenin believed that socialism could only be built in an advanced industrial economy.

Lenin's 'Soviet state'

In October 1917, Lenin seized power on behalf of the Soviets. The October Revolution formally handed power to the All-Russian Congress of Soviets, which met in Petrograd in October 1917. The Congress created **Sovnarkom**, a new government to replace the **Provisional Government**. Lenin was elected as the first head of the new government.

Lenin's first government passed a series of **decrees** that were genuinely popular. They included:
- the Decree on Land, which gave peasants the right to seize land from the **nobility** and the Church
- the Decree of Peace, which committed the new government to withdrawing from the First World War and seeking peace
- Workers' Decrees (November 1917) established an eight-hour maximum working day and a minimum wage.

Civil War, 1918–21

For the first few months, Sovnarkom had little real power outside Petrograd and Moscow. The Russian Civil War allowed Lenin to establish Communist control over the whole of Russia.

The Civil War radically changed the nature of the Communist government; it led to the emergence of an **authoritarian**, **centralised** and **bureaucratic regime**.

The Russian Civil War

The Civil War raged from mid-1918 to early 1921, ending in Communist victory. There were a number of different groups fighting during the Russian Civil War.
- The Reds: Communist forces
- The Whites: liberals, Tsarists or those who wanted to establish a military dictatorship.
- The 'Greens': associated with the Left Socialist Revolutionaries (SRs) or anarchist groups. They fought for the **autonomy** of local groups of peasants.

Political centralisation

Centralisation of power was Lenin's prime method of ensuring victory. During the Civil War power passed from Sovnarkom, which was technically accountable to the Soviets, to the **Politburo** – the most powerful committee of the highly centralised Communist Party.

Bureaucracy

The new government also became increasingly **bureaucratic**. The government relied on the skills of administrators to run the economy and the army during the Civil War. Therefore, the Communist *nomenklatura* who dominated the government were educated members of the former middle class, economists, statisticians, and engineers, who had worked for the Tsar's government.

Authoritarianism

Lenin and the Communists had promised a radically democratic regime. However, they used terror and repression against their opponents (see page 40). In February 1921 Lenin went further and authorised the **Cheka** (see page 42) to destroy the remaining opposition political parties.

! Complete the paragraph

Below are a sample exam question and a paragraph written in answer to this question. The paragraph contains a point and specific examples, but lacks a concluding analytical link back to the question. Complete the paragraph adding this link in the space provided.

> How accurate is it to say that the Communist government became increasingly centralised in the period 1918–28?

The Communist government clearly became increasingly centralised during the Civil War. First, Lenin was able to extend Communist control. Autonomous areas that had been controlled locally by the Left SRs or other peasant groups, known as 'Greens', were conquered by the Red Army and then brought under control of the central government. Additionally, Lenin's decision to control Russia through the Politburo rather than through Sovnarkom led to increasing centralisation. The Politburo was the highest committee of the centrally controlled Communist Party. Therefore,

_____

_____

⚡ Spot the mistake   a

Below are a sample exam question and a paragraph written in answer to this question. Why does this paragraph not get into Level 4? Once you have identified the mistake, rewrite the paragraph so that it displays the qualities of Level 4. The mark scheme on page 99 will help you.

> How far was political centralisation the main consequence of Communist government in the Soviet Union in the years 1918–28?

In 1917 Lenin and the Communists seized power in a revolution. Lenin created a one-party state and a Communist dictatorship. Lenin was a Communist who wanted to create a socialist society, which was different from capitalism. He was influenced by the German philosopher Karl Marx. Lenin tried to establish a 'Soviet state' based on local Soviets and Sovnarkom. This led to a Civil War between 1918 and 1921, which was the Communist Reds against other forces known as the Whites and the Greens. By 1921 the Communists had won and Lenin had created a centralised state. It was also a one-party state as the Communists were the only party allowed.

The nature of government under Lenin

The nature of the Communist Party changed radically during the Civil War. Lenin had constantly argued that the abolition of democracy was a temporary measure in order to win the Civil War. However, after the Communists had achieved victory Lenin introduced a series of measures that restricted democracy further.

The Party congress of 1921

The Party congress of 1921 addressed the crisis created by the Civil War. First, **War Communism** (see page 20) had created a famine. Secondly, the **Red Terror** (see page 42) led to a backlash against Communist repression.

- From the autumn of 1920 peasants in Tambov rebelled against War Communism and Cheka brutality. By January 1921 a rebel force of 50,000 was fighting the Communists across the whole Tambov region.
- In early 1921 there was a wave of strikes across Russia's main cities. In Petrograd the Red Army responded by opening fire on unarmed workers.
- Sailors at the Kronstadt naval base rebelled against Communist brutality. The mutineers demanded an end to War Communism, and a restoration of democracy.

At the party congress of 1921 Lenin responded by replacing War Communism with the **New Economic Policy (NEP)**. However, he continued to persecute other political parties and refused to allow a return to democracy.

The ban on factions

Lenin also faced opposition within the Communist Party from two **factions**:

- the Workers' Opposition wanted to reintroduce workers' control of industry
- the Democratic Centralists wanted to make the Communist Party more democratic.

Lenin responded by tightening Communist political control. Lenin introduced a **resolution**, 'On Party Unity', which banned factions inside the Party. Party members found guilty of forming factions could be expelled from the Party as punishment. The ban on factions helped strengthen Lenin's position within the party by making opposition to his policies more difficult to organise. Nonetheless, there was still debate within the Party on key issues such as economic policy.

Lenin's legacy

Lenin died in 1924, leaving a highly authoritarian political legacy. Lenin succeeded in creating a dictatorship of the proletariat to defend the revolution. However, he destroyed soviet democracy and replaced it with a one-party state.

Decline of Sovnarkom

Lenin did not abolish Sovnarkom. Rather, it simply ceased to function as the main centre of government. From 1920, the Politburo effectively became the Government of Russia. Sovnarkom played a much smaller role, merely approving the decisions that had already been made by the Politburo.

The 'party-state'

By 1921, the new government was based on two parallel structures: the Communist Party, and the Soviet state. From 1921 opposition parties were formally banned. Consequently, the Communist Party dominated the Soviets creating a new form of government that became known as the 'party-state'.

A new elite

The Civil War also changed the nature of the Communist Party. In 1918 the Communist Party was a group of workers and revolutionaries. By 1921 the Party became increasingly dominated by administrators from the former middle class. Moreover, the Party used its power to ensure that Communist Party members received more food and better accommodation than ordinary workers. By the early 1920s it was clear that although the Communist Party claimed to rule on behalf of the workers, it was becoming a privileged new elite.

Identify the concept a

Below are five sample exam questions based on some of the following concepts:

- cause – questions concern the reasons for something, or why something happened
- consequence – questions concern the impact of an event, an action or a policy
- change/continuity – questions ask you to investigate the extent to which things changed or stayed the same
- similarity/difference – questions ask you to investigate the extent to which two events, actions or policies were similar
- significance – questions concern the importance of an event, an action or a policy.

Read each of the questions and work out which of the concepts they are based on.

1 How accurate is it to say that there were major changes in the role of the Communist Party in the years 1918–28?

2 Was Lenin's ideology the main reason for the creation of a one-party state in the USSR in the years 1918–28? Explain your answer. **AS**

3 To what extent was Lenin responsible for the growing centralisation of Communist government in the years 1918–28?

4 Was the creation of a one-party state the main consequence of Communist government in the years 1918–28? Explain your answer. **AS**

5 How far do you agree that the Civil War was the most significant factor in the centralisation of Communist power in the years 1918–28?

Identify key terms a

Below is a sample Section A question, which includes a key word or term. Key terms are important because their meaning can be helpful in structuring your answer, developing an argument, and establishing criteria that will help form the basis of a judgement.

> How accurate is it to say that there were major changes in the role of the Communist Party in the years 1918–28?

- First, identify the key word or term. This will be a word or phrase that is important to the meaning of the question. Underline the word or phrase.
- Secondly, define the key phrase. Your definition should set out the key features of the phrase or word that you are defining.
- Third, make an essay plan that reflects your definition.
- Finally, write a sentence answering the question that refers back to the definition.

Now repeat the task, and consider how the change in key terms affects the structure, argument and final judgement of your essay.

> To what extent was Lenin responsible for the growing centralisation of Communist government in the years 1918–28?

Stalin in power, 1928–53

Between 1928 and 1953 **Stalin** transformed the government of the Soviet Union. Through a series of violent purges, known as the **Great Terror**, Stalin created a personal dictatorship.

The elimination of opponents

Between 1923 and 1928, Stalin was engaged in a struggle for power against **Trotsky**, **Bukharin** and **Zinoviev**. In order to win, Stalin used a series of tactics.

- Stalin had to establish that he, rather than the other contenders, was a true Leninist. This changed the nature of the Party by establishing a new ideological orthodoxy.
- Stalin also established dominance over the Politburo. Under Lenin members of the Politburo had been free to debate policies. Stalin expelled his main rivals from the Politburo and packed it with his supporters.
- Stalin also used patronage to win support in the party. As **General Secretary**, Stalin could give well paid and powerful jobs to his supporters. Equally, as head of the **Rabkrin** he had the power to investigate and, if necessary, sack Party members and government officials. Stalin's power to promote and sack Party members meant that Stalin could count on the loyalty of Party members who wanted to retain their positions or get a promotion.
- It established the principle that Stalin had the right to use terror against anyone who was disloyal.

These techniques that Stalin used in the 1920s continued to be the basis of his dominance throughout his rule.

The Purges of the 1930s

The Purges of the 1930s consolidated Stalin's hold on power.

Causes

By 1928, Stalin was undisputed leader of the Communist Party and the Soviet Union. At that time, he expelled Trotsky from the Communist Party and the Soviet Union and placed Zinoviev under **house arrest**. Nonetheless, the Party was still full of people who had supported Stalin's rivals. Consequently, Stalin feared that he would lose power. Moreover, Stalin's economic policies (see pages 24–26) had created economic chaos, and **Sergei Kirov**, head of the Communist Party in **Leningrad**, had emerged as a popular figure within the Party.

Extent

Stalin responded to these perceived threats by launching the Great Terror, or Great Purge, a campaign of arrests, torture, mass imprisonments and executions that finally removed his opponents. The Great Terror was at its height from 1935 to 1938. It was responsible for the deaths of around 10 million Soviet citizens, approximately 10 per cent of the population.

Political consequences

The Great Terror finally eliminated Stalin's old rivals. The most public aspect of the Great Terror was the three **Show Trials** that took place in 1936, 1937 and 1938. They led to the humiliation and execution of Zinoviev, Bukharin and Trotsky's main supporters.

At a deeper level, the Great Terror led to the death or imprisonment of a whole generation of Communists who had known and worked with Lenin. This allowed Stalin to appoint a new generation of Party leaders who owed their positions to him, and who were therefore loyal to Stalin alone.

By the mid-1930s Stalin's position was wholly secure.

Personal dictatorship

The Great Terror led to an important change in Soviet government. Lenin had ruled through the Communist Party and had allowed debate at the top of the Party. Indeed, he worked with a range of Communists such as Bukharin and Trotsky who had radically different visions.

Stalin terrorised the Communist Party. This ended Party rule and established the personal rule of Stalin. Under Stalin, the Communist Party and the state had very limited authority. By 1935 neither Party nor state could oppose Stalin.

! Delete as applicable

Below are a sample exam question and an introduction to an essay written in answer to this question. Read the paragraph and decide which of the possible options (in bold) is most appropriate. Delete the least appropriate options and complete the paragraph by justifying your selection.

How far did the fundamental features of Communist government change in the years 1921–53?

The fundamental features of Communist government changed **greatly/moderately/ to a very limited extent** in the years 1921–53. Some of the fundamental features of Communist government, such as the one-party state, political centralisation and authoritarianism remained in place. However, under Stalin, the government of the Party changed as Stalin established personal rule. Therefore, fundamental features of Communist government changed **greatly/moderately/to a very limited extent** because

_____

_____

↕ Support or challenge?

Below is a sample exam question, which asks how far you agree with a specific statement. Below this is a series of general statements, which are relevant to the question. Using your own knowledge and the information on the opposite page decide whether these statements support or challenge the statement in the question and tick the appropriate box.

How far do you agree that the elimination of Stalin's opponents was the principal reason for the development of personal rule in the years 1928–53?

	SUPPORT	CHALLENGE
Lenin created a one-party state.		
Lenin created a highly centralised government.		
Stalin had important roles within the Party and government.		
The Moscow Show Trials eliminated Stalin's main opponents.		
Stalin's terror eliminated his opponents throughout the government.		

Stalin's power over Party and state

Stalin created a new form of government based on his total power over the Party and the state.

Totalitarianism

Many historians argue that Stalin constructed a new kind of dictatorship based on:
- complete control of the economy (see pages 24–26)
- use of widespread political terror to eliminate his opponents (see page 42)
- complete control of the media (see page 36)
- use of extensive propaganda to win the hearts and minds of his people (see page 36).

Stalin's dictatorship also had different aims from previous dictatorships. Whereas dictators such as the Tsar had been content with the absence of opposition, Stalin demanded heartfelt enthusiasm from his people. In that sense, Stalin did not simply want obedience, but also the full commitment of his people.

The relationship between Party and state

Stalin inherited the Communist Party and the Soviet state from Lenin. Lenin had created both, but had failed to define their relationship. Stalin used the vagueness of the relationship between the Party and the state to his advantage by encouraging competition between the two bodies.

Rivalry

Stalin promoted rivals to similar positions in the Party and the state. For example, he placed Andrei Zhdanov, **Beria**'s key rival, in charge of Party supervision of Beria's political police. Encouraging competition between Party and state officials meant that senior officials in the Soviet government competed with each other and not with Stalin.

Shifting powerbases

Stalin also shifted power from the Party to the state.
- In 1938 the Politburo was the most senior committee in government.
- By 1942, the State Defence Committee was the most powerful committee in government.
- After the Second World War the Council of Ministers, another committee in the Soviet state, became more powerful.

By shifting the centre of power within the government, Stalin was able to ensure that none of these senior committees grew to rival him. Equally, Stalin ensured that he was the only person involved with all of these top committees. Therefore, he was the only leader with an overview of the entire government.

The Soviet Union and the Second World War

The Second World War began in Western Europe in 1939 between nations including Germany, Britain and France. The Soviet Union became involved following German invasion in 1941. Subsequently, it allied with Britain and the USA, forming the Grand Alliance against Nazi Germany and Fascist Italy. The War in Europe ended with an Allied victory in May 1945.

Renewed terror

A final way in which Stalin held on to power was the continued use of terror. By purging hundreds of Party and state officials in his last years he inspired fear in thousands more.
- The Leningrad Affair of 1949 was a purge of the Leningrad Party. Stalin was concerned that Andrei Zhdanov had created an independent powerbase in Russia's second city. Following Zhdanov's death around 100 of his supporters were shot and 2,000 arrested and dismissed.
- Stalin also used persecution to test the loyalty of his senior ministers. For example, in 1949 Stalin ordered the imprisonment of Vyacheslav Molotov's wife. **Molotov** had been a member of the Politburo since 1926 and was one of Stalin's closest allies. Molotov demonstrated his loyalty to Stalin by doing nothing to win his wife's freedom.

Stalin's legacy

On Stalin's death in 1953, the Soviet state and the Communist Party had been completely subordinated to Stalin. Neither Party nor state had any independent authority.

Simple essay style

Below is a sample exam question. Use your own knowledge and the information on the opposite page to produce a plan for this question. Choose four general points, and provide three pieces of specific information to support each general point. Once you have planned your essay, write the introduction and conclusion for the essay. The introduction should list the points to be discussed in the essay. The conclusion should summarise the key points and justify which point was the most important.

> To what extent was Lenin responsible for the emergence of a totalitarian government in the Soviet Union in the years 1918–53?

 ## Eliminate irrelevance

Below are a sample exam question and a paragraph written in answer to this question. Read the paragraph and identify parts of the paragraph that are not directly relevant to the question. Draw a line through the information that is irrelevant and justify your deletions in the margin.

> How far did the essential features of Communist government change in the period 1921–53?

One of the essential features of Communist government that changed dramatically between 1921 and 1953 was the power of the Communist Party. The Communist Party seized power in 1917 as a result of the October Revolution. By 1921 the Communist Party controlled the government. While Party rule was centralised and authoritarian, there was still debate within the Communist Party. Indeed, even after the ban on factions, debate continued over key issues such as economic policy. This changed significantly under Stalin. During Stalin's rise to power Stalin criticised his opponents for not being true Leninists. All Communists were influenced by the thought of the German philosopher Karl Marx. During the 1930s Stalin's terror attacked Communists with different views. This changed the nature of the Party significantly, by establishing a new ideological orthodoxy, which effectively ended freedom of debate in the Communist Party.

Khrushchev's attempts to reform government

Khrushchev emerged as leader of the Soviet Union by 1956. Khrushchev wanted to revive the Communist Party. However, reform threatened to destabilise the government. Therefore, Khrushchev was continually caught between stability and reform.

De-Stalinisation

Khrushchev wanted to preserve what he saw as the essential features of Communist government. However, he was also committed to **de-Stalinisation**:
- ending personal rule
- ending the use of terror.

De-Stalinisation took place in a series of stages.

Ending terror

Ending terror began immediately after Stalin's death.
- In March and April 1953 there were amnesties for various classes of prisoners.
- In May, 4,620 Communist prisoners were **rehabilitated**.

Personnel changes

Khrushchev removed Stalin loyalists from senior Party bodies. Between 1953 and 1956 Khrushchev replaced around half of the regional Party secretaries and 44 per cent of the **Central Committee**.

The Secret Speech

In 1956 Khrushchev criticised Stalin at the Party Congress. His speech was kept secret, as Khrushchev recognised that criticising Stalin risked undermining the authority of the Communist Party.

Khrushchev argued that Stalin had abandoned Party government and established a dictatorship based on the **'cult of personality'** (see page 38).

The impact of the Secret Speech

Stalin was widely loved in the Party. Therefore, many Communists were profoundly shocked. As news of the Secret Speech was leaked, there were demonstrations in favour of multi-party democracy at Moscow State University. Khrushchev responded by backtracking. He agreed with his critics that the Soviet people were 'not ready' to know the truth about Stalin.

Democratisation and decentralisation

Even so, Khrushchev introduced major government reforms.
- 'Democratisation' was designed to allow workers and peasants to join the Communist Party. Membership grew from 6.9 million in 1954 to 11 million in 1964. In this sense, the Party became more representative of the people of Russia as, by 1964, 60 per cent of its members were either workers or peasants.
- 'Decentralisation' entailed the abolition of some central ministries. Economic powers were then devolved to 105 newly created economic councils. Additionally, he moved the Ministry of Agriculture away from Moscow to make it 'closer to the fields'.

Backlash

Khrushchev's reforms meant that many Communist officials were demoted, or lost their jobs. Consequently, there was renewed criticism of Khrushchev within the Party. In 1957 the 'Anti-Party group' attempted to oust Khrushchev. However, Khrushchev survived due to the support of the Central Committee.

Khrushchev's final reforms

The Twenty-Second Party Congress of October 1961 introduced Khrushchev's final major political reforms.
- The Party was divided in two: one party supervised agriculture, the other industry.
- Fixed terms were introduced for all government jobs, forcing Party officials to move jobs regularly. Central Committee members had a fixed term of 16 years. Khrushchev hoped this would stop the party **stagnating**.

The extent of de-Stalinisation

Some aspects of Stalinism lived on. The government never publicly rejected his legacy, or admitted the extent of Stalin's crimes. Nonetheless, Khrushchev succeeded in ending the use of terror against party officials.

Khrushchev also successfully ended Stalin's system of personal rule. Unlike Stalin, Khrushchev was forced to negotiate with other senior figures in the Party. Indeed, the growing power of the Party lead to Khrushchev's downfall. In October 1964 Khrushchev was forced to retire by senior figures in the Party who believed that his reforms had gone too far.

(i) Identify an argument

Below are a series of definitions, a sample exam question and two sample conclusions. One of the conclusions achieves a high mark because it contains an argument. The other achieves a lower mark because it contains only description and assertion. Identify which is which. The mark scheme on page 99 will help you.

Description: a detailed account.

Assertion: a statement of fact or an opinion which is not supported by a reason.

Reason: a statement which explains or justifies something.

Argument: an assertion justified with a reason.

How accurate is it to say that Khrushchev's reforms transformed the nature of Soviet government in the years 1956–64?

In conclusion, Khrushchev's reforms transformed the nature of Soviet government because they ended the key features of Stalinism. Khrushchev ended both personal rule and the use of terror against the Communist Party. At the same time, he revitalised the Party by allowing greater freedom for debate and by allowing a new generation of workers to join. Not all of Khrushchev's reforms created significant change. Indeed, the government remained centralised and undemocratic. Nonetheless, Khrushchev's de-Stalinisation genuinely transformed the government. Indeed, Khrushchev removing the essential features of Stalinism to such an extent that the Party was able to force Khrushchev to retire, which would have been unthinkable under Stalin.

Khrushchev undoubtedly made changes to the government introducing policies such as democratisation and de-Stalinisation. However, these did not end Communist Party dominance within government. Equally, his policy of decentralisation failed to alter the centralised nature of the government.

Overall, Khrushchev's reforms transformed the nature of Soviet government to an extent. Khrushchev achieved some de-Stalinisation by ending personal rule, and ending the use of terror. He also introduced policies such as democratisation, decentralisation, and fixed terms to reform the government. Nonetheless, the government continued to be dominated by the Communist Party.

(i) Turning assertion into argument

Below are a sample exam question and a series of assertions. Read the exam question and then add a justification to each of the assertions to turn it into an argument.

How far did Communist government in the USSR change in the years 1928–64?

Khrushchev's reforms led to a significant change in some aspects of Soviet government because

_____

Communist government was not totally transformed in these years because

_____

De-Stalinisation was the most significant reform in the years 1928–64 because

_____

There were small changes in Communist government in the last years of Stalin's rule because

_____

Stability and stagnation under Brezhnev, 1964–82

Following Khrushchev, government effectively ended reform. **Brezhnev** believed that the revolution had been completed by Lenin and Stalin. Therefore, he argued that the Party needed to resist change and should focus instead on 'stability'.

Restoration

Brezhnev reversed Khrushchev's key reforms in a process called 'restoration'.
- He reversed decentralisation, re-establishing the **all-union** ministries that Khrushchev had abolished.
- He ended the split between industrial and agricultural wings of the Party.

Stability of cadres

Brezhnev abolished many of Khrushchev's reforms. Specifically, he reversed fixed-term positions. However, there was not a return to Stalinist terror. Rather, Brezhnev controlled the Party by offering Party members security. Brezhnev's policy 'stability of **cadres**' discouraged demotions or changes in personnel within government, ensuring job security for Party members.

Political stagnation, 1970–85

Restoration led to a period of political stagnation.

Gerontocracy

The stability of cadres meant that government officials stayed in the same job for years. As a result, few young people entered the government and the average age of government officials increased. Indeed, between 1964 and 1971 only two people were promoted to the Politburo. The average age of people on the Politburo rose from 58 in 1966 to 75 in 1982. Brezhnev's style of government was nicknamed a gerontocracy: rule of old people.

Inefficiency

As the government aged, it became less effective. Under Brezhnev there were extremely limited opportunities for promotion. Consequently, officials were effectively stuck in dead-end jobs with few opportunities for advancement. As a result, 'stability of cadres' provided no incentives for hard work, because there were so few opportunities for promotion.

Corruption

Under Brezhnev sackings were rare. Career development and options for progression were also extremely limited. This created the context for huge corruption. Soviet officials, who could not grow rich through hard work and promotion, used their positions to grow rich, knowing they were unlikely to be disciplined.

One form of corruption was to sell luxury goods on the **black market**. Brezhnev was implicated in the corruption. His daughter Galina Brezhneva was able to get access to diamonds. One of her lovers smuggled millions of pounds' worth of diamonds out of the USSR. He was eventually prosecuted after Brezhnev's death.

Moral decline

Brezhnev's rule also led to a change in the character of government. Under Lenin, Stalin and Khrushchev Soviet government had followed a utopian vision. These leaders had encouraged the Soviet people to work hard in order to build socialism. Brezhnev believed that the job was done. He talked about revolution in other parts of the world, such as Zimbabwe, Mexico and Peru, but he no longer encouraged revolutionary spirit at home.

As a result, the Soviet people became increasingly cynical, for while Brezhnev argued that socialism had been achieved the majority of Russians realised there were major problems of corruption and stagnation in the Soviet Union.

Andropov and Chernenko (1982–85)

Following the death of Brezhnev the Soviet Union was ruled by **Yuri Andropov** and **Konstantin Chernenko**. Both had been close to Brezhnev and therefore they rejected reform. Nonetheless, Andropov initiated policies that were designed to end corruption and increase efficiency.
- He abandoned the 'stability of cadres' policy, replacing a quarter of senior officials,
- His most important initiative was an anti-corruption campaign.

The anti-corruption campaign attacked senior figures such as Red Army generals and **Minister of the Interior** Nikolai Shchelokov. He also prosecuted 'Boris the Gypsy', Brezhnev's daughter's lover.

Chernenko was also unwilling to consider major reform. Due to ill health and the brevity of his rule he achieved very little as Soviet leader.

Develop the detail

Below are a sample exam question and a paragraph written in answer to this question. The paragraph contains a limited amount of detail. Annotate the paragraph to add additional detail to the answer.

How far did Soviet government change in the years 1953–85?

Brezhnev introduced a great deal of change in government in his early years. He reversed a lot of reforms. He also introduced new policies to help stabilise the government. Over time, this meant that the nature of government also changed. In this way, there were significant changes in government under Brezhnev, as Brezhnev reversed Khrushchev's reforms and creating stability also changed the nature of government in the long run.

 Developing an argument

Below are a sample exam question, a list of key points to be made in the essay, and a paragraph from the essay. Read the question, the plan and the sample paragraph. Rewrite the paragraph in order to develop an argument. Your paragraph should answer the question directly, and set out the evidence that supports your argument. Crucially, it should develop an argument by setting out a general answer to the question and reasons that support this.

How far do you agree that the nature of government under Brezhnev was radically different from government under Khrushchev?

Key points:
- Brezhnev's prime goal was stability, whereas Khrushchev wanted reform.
- Brezhnev's government was stagnant and corrupt, whereas Khrushchev introduced policies to make the party more open and dynamic.
- Both Brezhnev and Khrushchev were committed to one-party rule.
- Both Brezhnev and Khrushchev abandoned terror as a way of managing the Party.

The nature of government under Brezhnev was different from government under Khrushchev to some extent. Brezhnev's government was different from Khrushchev's as his prime goal was stability, whereas Khrushchev wanted reform. Also Brezhnev's government was stagnant and corrupt, whereas Khrushchev introduced policies to make the Party more open and dynamic. However, there were also similarities. Both Brezhnev and Khrushchev were committed to one-party rule. Moreover, both Brezhnev and Khrushchev abandoned terror as a way of managing the Party.

Exam focus

Below is a sample high-level essay. Read it and the comments around it. The answer refers to the cult of personality, which is dealt with on page 38.

How far did Soviet government change in the years 1921–53?

There were important changes in the Soviet government in the years 1921–41. However, many of the key features of Soviet government were already in place by 1921. In order to answer the question, I will consider the nature of Communist government, the use of terror, and the role of the leader.

The essay begins with a clear focus on the question.

The nature of Communist government changed very little between 1921 and 1953. By 1921 the Communist government was highly centralised, bureaucratic and authoritarian. Communism continued to be centralised, bureaucratic and authoritarian until 1953. By 1921, Lenin relied heavily on the Communist Party and the government officials, or *nomenklatura,* to run the government. Stalin did the same. Indeed, Stalin relied on the support of the *nomenklatura,* whose power had grown under Lenin since 1918. The Communist Party continued to be highly centralised. Lenin had introduced the ban on factions in 1921 to increase central control. Stalin took this further by eliminating his opponents Trotsky, Bukharin and Zinoviev and their supporters in the Great Terror. This also supports the idea that the Soviet government continued to be authoritarian, as, under Lenin, the government refused to tolerate popular debate, something that continued under Stalin. Nonetheless, it could be argued that there was a change. Although the nature of Communist rule did not change, the extent of centralisation, bureaucracy and authoritarianism changed. For example, Lenin tolerated discussion within the Party to a much greater extent than Stalin, and Lenin relied on the Party, whereas centralisation went further under Stalin through the creation of personal rule. In this way, while the nature of Soviet government did not change, government did change because it became more centralised, bureaucratic and authoritarian under Stalin.

The introduction sets out the key features of Soviet government that it will evaluate.

The first main paragraph discusses three main aspects of Soviet government.

The essay uses technical vocabulary to show knowledge of the period.

The essay concludes by evaluating the extent of change. The evaluation is based on a distinction between the nature and the extent of the key features discussed in the paragraph.

The use of terror was one of the most significant changes in government in the period 1921 to 1953. Lenin used terror extensively. For example, in 1921 he ordered the ruthless destruction of the mutiny in the Kronstadt naval base, and the brutal suppression of the peasant rebellion across the whole Tambov region. Moreover, he also used the Cheka to destroy opposition political parties. However, Lenin never used terror against the Communist Party. He disagreed with radicals such as the Workers' Opposition, who wanted to reintroduce workers' control of industry, and the Democratic Centralists, who wanted to make the Communist Party more democratic, and he banned their factions, but their leaders remained in government. Stalin, by contrast, used terror against his opponents within the Communist Party. The Moscow Show Trials led to the execution of Zinoviev, Bukharin and Trotsky's main supporters. Moreover, the Terror led to the death or imprisonment of a whole generation of Communists. Indeed, it was responsible for the deaths of around 10 million Soviet citizens, approximately 10 per cent of the population. The use of terror was one of the most significant changes in government in the period 1921 to 1953 because Lenin restricted his use of terror to enemies outside the Party, whereas Stalin extended the use of terror and used it as a weapon against the Communist Party.

The essay uses a range of detail to support its points.

Finally, the biggest change in Soviet government in the years 1921 to 1953 was the role of the leader. By 1921, Lenin's government was based firmly on the Communist Party. The Communist Party Congresses still made important decisions, and there was considerable disagreement within the Party on important issues. Indeed, Lenin consistently faced opposition within the Communist Party. Lenin certainly tightened his control with the 1921 ban on factions, but he never created a personal dictatorship. Stalin, by contrast, ended Party rule and established personal rule. Under Stalin, the Communist Party and the state had very limited authority. He was able to sustain personal rule by continually shifting the centre of his power. Between 1921 and 1938 the Politburo was the centre of government. However, by 1942 Stalin ruled through the State Defence Committee. Finally, after 1945 he ruled through the Council of Ministers. Shifting powerbases kept Stalin strong, and the Party weak, because the Party was never able to consolidate its position. This was a major change in Soviet government because Lenin always worked to strengthen the Party, whereas Stalin always worked to strengthen his own position.

This paragraph concludes with a judgement based on clear criteria: the extent to which Stalin carried on with Lenin's principles.

In conclusion, while the nature of Communist government stayed similar, the extent of centralisation, bureaucracy, authoritarianism and terror all increased under Stalin. The biggest change was the establishment of personal rule, because, unlike other changes, it went against Lenin's principles. Lenin was prepared to use terror, but never against the Party, and Lenin did not seek to establish personal rule. In both these senses there was a major change in Communist government, because Stalin governed in a way that reflected his personal desire for power rather than Lenin's principles.

The conclusion uses the same criteria to reach an overall judgement.

This essay achieves a mark in Level 5 because it evaluates the extent of change through analysing a range of the key features of Soviet government. It is based on a sufficient range and depth of knowledge to answer the question. It develops a clear logical argument and uses valid criteria to substantiate an overall judgement.

Reverse engineering

The best essays are based on careful plans. Read the essay and the comments and try to work out the general points of the plan used to write the essay. Once you have done this, note down the specific examples used to support each general point.

AS Level questions

Was Communist ideology the main reason for changes in government in the years 1918–53? Explain your answer.

How significant was de-Stalinisation in the changes in government in the years 1953–85?

To what extent did the power of the Communist Party grow in the years 1953–85?

To what extent were there changes in Communist government in the years 1953–85?

Was the Russian Civil War the main reason for the centralisation of government in the years 1918–53?

2 Industrial and agricultural change, 1917–85

Lenin's economy, 1918–21

Lenin, like all Marxists, believed that an economic revolution was essential to **building socialism**. Lenin had a variety of economic objectives.

- Modernisation: he believed socialism required the construction of a highly advanced economy.
- Consolidation: he needed economic stability to help retain his hold on power.
- Military victory: he needed the economy to supply the Red Army during the Civil War.
- Destroy capitalism: Lenin wanted to create an economy that was more efficient than capitalism and ended inequality.

Lenin's different priorities shaped the evolution of his economic policy. Often Lenin had to put immediate **pragmatic** goals above long-term **ideological** goals.

Marx and the economy

One of the key problems facing Lenin was that Marx had not set out a detailed description of how a socialist economy would work. Marx argued that a socialist economy would be highly advanced and organised according to 'a common plan', but argued that it was impossible to describe the future in detail.

The nationalisation of industry

From March 1918 Lenin began the **nationalisation** of industry. Nationalisation was at the heart of Lenin's economic policy from 1918 to 1924.

State capitalism

In March 1918 Lenin also introduced state capitalism. Lenin argued that it was an economic phase between capitalism and socialism. State capitalism was based on the nationalisation of large-scale industry. Nationalisation ended capitalism by passing the ownership of industry from capitalists to the new state.

Lenin hoped that nationalisation would lead to greater efficiency as the government could employ experts to run the economy. Control of the nationalised industries was then centralised by the **Vesenkha**, which would:

- re-establish worker discipline by offering higher pay to productive workers

- ensure factories were properly managed by placing them under the control of well-paid specialists
- co-ordinate economic production to meet the needs of new society.

War Communism

State capitalism was always intended to be a temporary measure. The start of the Civil War in the summer of 1918 led to the introduction of a series of emergency economic measures. Together these became known as War Communism. Their goal was to ensure Communist victory in the Civil War.

War Communism entailed the following measures.

- The nationalisation of all industry.
- food dictatorship: the free market in food was abolished. Grain was forcibly requisitioned from the peasants, and food was rationed by the Supply Commissariat. Workers and soldiers got the largest rations; the smallest rations were given to members of the **bourgeoisie**.
- Labour discipline: Lenin introduced an 11-hour working day, and compulsory work for all able-bodied men aged 16 to 50.
- The abolition of the market: money became worthless due to **hyperinflation**, and was then formally abolished. Private trade was made illegal.

The consequences of War Communism

War Communism led to military victory, but economic ruin.

War Communism destroyed incentives to work, as peasants and workers were not rewarded for their labour. Consequently, there was an economic catastrophe.

- By 1920 there was a famine in the countryside. The 1921 harvest was only 46 per cent of the 1913 harvest, which led to the deaths of around 6 million people.
- Additionally, workers fled the cities in search of food. In total, the industrial workforce declined from 2.6 million workers in 1917 to 1.2 million in early 1921.

The economic crisis of 1921 led to major economic reform: the New Economic Policy.

Mind map

Use the information on the opposite page, and the information on Lenin's government on page 22 to add detail to the mind map below.

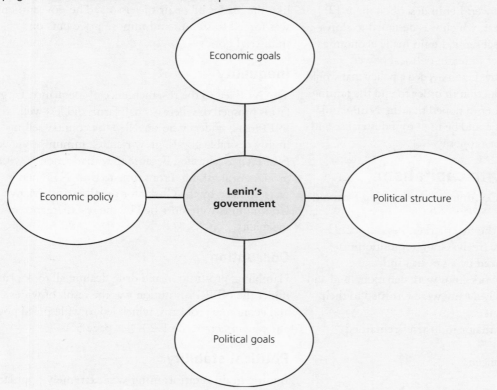

Spot the mistake

a

Below are a sample exam question and a paragraph written in answer to this question. Why does this paragraph not get into Level 4? Once you have identified the mistake, rewrite the paragraph so that it displays the qualities of Level 4. The mark scheme on page 99 will help you.

How successful was Communist economic policy in the years 1918–28?

Communist economic policy was successful in the sense that it met its immediate military goals in the years 1918–28. War Communism helped the Communists win the Civil War (1918–21) through nationalisation of all industry and labour discipline in the factories. War Communism also contributed to Communist victory as it introduced a food dictatorship based on forcible grain requisitioning from the peasants, and food rationing. This was organised by the Supply Commissariat, and ensured that workers and soldiers got the largest rations. These policies met the Communists' immediate military goal of winning the Civil War.

Lenin introduced the New Economic Policy (NEP) for a variety of reasons.

- To retain political power: Lenin described the NEP as an economic retreat, which was designed to stop a political defeat. In that sense, Lenin made economic compromises in order to retain political power.
- To revive the economy: Lenin needed a policy that would stimulate grain production in order to end the famine.
- To build socialism: Lenin hoped that the NEP would generate wealth that could be used to industrialise and modernise the Soviet economy.

Compromise with capitalism

The NEP ended War Communism by creating a **mixed economy**.

- Farming was left to the free market. Peasants could buy, sell and produce freely. Grain requisitioning ended and was replaced by a **tax in kind**.
- Small factories and workshops were denationalised and allowed to trade freely. Many were returned to their former capitalist owners.
- Large factories and major industries remained nationalised.
- Money was reintroduced.

The consequences of the NEP

The NEP led to political and economic stability. However, it did not lead to rapid industrial growth. Nor was it wholly popular within the Party as it was a compromise with capitalism.

Farming

Ending grain requisitioning was extremely popular among the peasants. Free trade also encouraged peasants to grow more food. Therefore, the famine ended, and farming revived.

Industry

The NEP also led to industrial growth. Lenin authorised a major electrification campaign, which revived an industry that had effectively been destroyed by the Civil War. However, industrial recovery was slow.

The 'scissors crisis'

Agriculture recovered quickly; industry recovered much more slowly. This imbalance led to a fall in the price of food and a rise in the price of industrial goods. A gap opened up between farmers' incomes and industrial prices.

Trotsky nicknamed the crisis the 'scissors crisis', as the lines on the graph illustrating the problem looked like the blades of a pair of scissors. The government was forced to step in and impose price cuts on industrial goods.

Inequality

The NEP led to the re-emergence of inequality. Large farms prospered, whereas small farms did less well. 'NEPmen', traders who travelled the country selling highly desirable goods, grew rich. Communists viewed NEPmen as parasites, because they made money without producing anything. From time to time NEPmen were arrested by the Cheka for **profiteering**. Many Communists were horrified by the re-emergence of inequality.

Corruption

Gambling, prostitution and drug dealing all took place under the NEP. Prostitution was the result of wider social and economic problems, which led to widespread poverty among women in the 1920s (see page 56).

Political stability

Ending grain requisitioning was extremely popular among the peasants. Therefore, peasants began to support the regime. This was a deliberate part of Lenin's policy. Indeed, he argued that the Communist government was based on an alliance, or 'smychka', between the workers and the peasants, which was made possible by the NEP.

Divisions in the Party

The NEP also divided the Communist Party.

- The right-wing supported the NEP, arguing that it was a form of state capitalism, and a necessary transitional stage.
- The left-wing opposed the NEP, arguing that it was allowing the problems of capitalism to re-emerge.
- The centre supported the NEP, arguing that it was helping to rebuild the economy.

Delete as applicable

Below are a sample exam question and an introduction written in answer to this question. Read the paragraph and decide which of the possible options (in bold) is most appropriate. Delete the least appropriate options and complete the paragraph by justifying your selection.

How far do you agree that the Communist government faced severe economic challenges in the years 1918–28?

The Communist government faced economic challenges in the years 1918–28. These challenges were **severe/moderate/minor**. The Communists faced the economic challenge of the Civil War, the challenge of the Great Famine, the challenge of industrial development, and the economic problems created by the NEP in the 1920s. Therefore, the Communist government faced **severe/moderate/minor** economic challenges in the years 1918–28 because

_____

_____

_____

_____

Support or challenge?

Below is a sample exam question, which asks how far you agree with a specific statement. Below this is a series of general statements, which are relevant to the question. Using your own knowledge and the information on the opposite page decide whether these statements support or challenge the statement in the question and tick the appropriate box.

How far do you agree that the most significant influence on Communist economic policy in the years 1917 to 1928 was the need to retain political power?

	SUPPORT	CHALLENGE
Lenin introduced the NEP to appease the peasants.		
Lenin introduced the Decree on Land to win the support of the peasants.		
State capitalism was introduced to make the economy more efficient.		
War Communism's main goal was ensuring Communist victory.		
The NEP was a compromise with capitalism.		
Lenin's long-term goal was to build socialism.		

The Stalin era: the Five-Year Plans and industrial change, 1928–41   REVISED

Stalin's 'revolution from above', launched in 1928, transformed the Soviet economy. Stalin's revolution ended the NEP introducing a command economy.

The nature of Stalin's plans

Under Stalin industrialisation was achieved through a series of Five-Year Plans. The plans were formulated by Gosplan, and set targets for every factory, mine and workshop in the Soviet Union. The plans were accompanied by massive propaganda campaigns designed to inspire workers to support the new system.

Economic planning?

Stalin argued that he had created a 'planned economy'. However, his 'plans' were essentially lists of targets. No attempt was made to match resources to the country's needs. In this sense, Stalin's economy is better understood as a command economy: an economy where the government controls production.

Reasons for the plans

Stalin introduced the plans for a variety of reasons.
- Ideology: Stalin wanted to abolish the capitalist market, and lay the economic foundation for socialism.
- Economics: the NEP had failed to lead to further industrialisation.
- Military: Stalin argued that Russia had to industrialise in order to prepare for war with capitalist nations.
- Political: by abolishing capitalism, Stalin won the support of the Party's left-wing.

The aims of the plans

Stalin's primary economic aim was to build up heavy industry. Therefore, the government invested heavily in building new iron and steel factories, and establishing new coalmines and oil wells. From 1936, Stalin also prioritised rearmament.

Stalin's plan did not focus on consumer goods in order to maximum resources for heavy industry and the military.

Achievements to 1941

Stalin's first three Five-Year Plans succeeded in industrialising the Soviet Union.

Heavy industry

Heavy industry was the biggest success of the first three Five-Year Plans.
- Electricity output increased almost ten-fold.
- Coal and steel production went up almost five times.
- There was a three-fold increase in oil production.

Transport

Stalin's polices also led to the growth of the transport infrastructure:
- The Moscow Metro's first train lines opened in 1935.
- The Moscow–Volga Canal opened in 1937.

Labour productivity

During the first Five-Year Plan labour productivity was extremely low. Consequently, the government initiated the Stakhanovite movement:
- A propaganda campaign praised the work of coal miner Alexei Stakhanov, who mined 14 times his quota in a single shift.
- Stalin authorised a system of higher payments to reward the most productive workers.

As a result, productivity rose between 25 per cent and 50 per cent in Russia's major industries. Nonetheless, Soviet productivity continued to lag behind that of other industrialised nations such as the USA, Germany and France.

Rearmament

Rearmament was also a success. By 1940 one-third of government spending was devoted to the military. Moreover, the plans led to the successful construction of nine military aircraft factories between 1939 and 1941.

Quality

Production quality was often low because factory managers were rewarded for producing large quantities of material, regardless of the quality.

Efficiency

Stalin's economy was very inefficient. Gosplan did not make a plan for how to use the materials produced, and poor transport and poor co-ordination meant that around 40 per cent of what was produced was wasted.

The plans were also undermined by Gosplan's unrealistic targets:
- Gosplan officials often had no idea how big the factories they controlled were or how much they could produce.
- Industrial managers lied about production levels to avoid punishment.
- Falsified data made economic management even harder, as effective planning relies on accurate data.

Simple essay style

Below is a sample exam question. Use your own knowledge and the information on the opposite page to produce a plan for this question. Choose four general points, and provide three pieces of specific information to support each general point. Once you have planned your essay, write the introduction and conclusion for the essay. The introduction should list the points to be discussed in the essay. The conclusion should summarise the key points and justify which point was the most important.

How accurate is it to say that there was a radical difference in the economic policies of Lenin and Stalin in the years 1917–41?

Spectrum of importance

Below are a sample exam question and a list of general points, which could be used to answer the question. Use your own knowledge and the information on the opposite page to reach a judgement about the importance of these general points to the question posed. Write numbers on the spectrum below to indicate their relative importance. Having done this, write a brief justification of your placement, explaining why some of these factors are more important than others. The resulting diagram could form the basis of an essay plan.

How accurate is it to say that the principal reason for the survival of Communist rule in the Soviet Union in the years 1917–28 was the introduction of the NEP?

1   The NEP
2   War Communism
3   Political centralisation
4   The creation of a one-party state

Least important ⟵——————————————————————⟶ Most important

The Stalin era: Agricultural collectivisation and its impact REVISED

Between 1928 and 1941 Soviet agriculture was collectivised. Collectivisation was a process by which:

- Small farms were merged into large farms of anything between 20 and 150 families.
- Ownership of farms was taken over by the state.

The process was extremely violent and led to a massive decline in agricultural production.

The causes of collectivisation

Collectivisation had a series of causes.

- Ideology: under the NEP farming was essentially run in a capitalist way. Communists wanted to abolish capitalism by ending **private ownership** of farms.
- Economics: under the NEP the government collected a small tax on farms. Collectivisation allowed the government to take much more wealth from farms, which could be invested in industrialisation.
- Failure of the NEP: agricultural production fell in 1927, leading to food shortages in the cities.
- Political: introducing collectivisation allowed Stalin to win support from the left of the Communist Party.

The process of collectivisation

Collectivisation was introduced in late 1929. Farms were forcibly merged, and equipment taken from richer peasants and given to the poorer peasants.

Many peasants responded by destroying their crops, animals and machinery. The government executed or deported the **kulaks** who resisted collectivisation.

The consequences of collectivisation

Collectivisation led to a crisis in agriculture.

Falling production

Unrest in rural areas led to the destruction of:

- 17 million horses
- 26 million cattle
- 11 million pigs
- 60 million sheep and goats.

At the same time, grain production also decreased from 73.3 million tons in 1928 to 68.4 million tons in 1933.

Famine

Collectivisation also led to famine in Ukraine, where resistance to collectivisation was intense. Stalin punished Ukraine by seizing its grain and livestock. The result was a government-created famine between 1932 and 1933, which resulted in 5 million deaths.

Modernisation

Collectivisation was accompanied by a degree of modernisation. The government allowed farms to hire tractors from Machine Tractor Stations, which were set up across the country. The 75,000 tractors that they provided had a limited impact on Soviet farming. At best, they made up for all of the horses that were lost due to collectivisation.

Grain procurement

Collectivisation allowed the government to procure much more grain than the NEP. In 1928, the government procured 10.8 million tons of grain from the peasants. This had risen to 22.6 million tons in 1933. Grain exports also rose from less than 1 million tons in 1928 to 4.7 million tons in 1930 and 5 million tons in 1931.

Slow recovery

Soviet agriculture recovered slowly from collectivisation. Grain harvests were regularly smaller than they had been in the best years of the NEP. Low grain harvests were, in part, a result of the fact that collective farms were less productive than private farms. On average, private farms produced around 410 kilos of grain per hectare, whereas collective farms produced about 320 kilos per hectare. In short, prior to the Second World War collective farms were less productive than farms under the NEP.

① Develop the detail

Below are a sample exam question and a paragraph written in answer to this question. The paragraph contains a limited amount of detail. Annotate the paragraph to add additional detail to the answer.

How successful were government policies in promoting economic growth in the USSR in the years 1917–41?

Between 1917 and 1941 government policies were largely unsuccessful in promoting economic growth in terms of agriculture. The most successful policy for promoting agriculture was the NEP. Collectivisation was much less successful. The least successful policy for promoting agricultural development was War Communism. Overall, government policies were largely unsuccessful in promoting the development of agriculture because Soviet agriculture only grew substantially under the NEP; for the rest of the period agriculture grew slowly or declined.

① Introducing an argument

Below are an exam question, an essay plan and a basic introduction and conclusion. Rewrite the introduction and conclusion so that they contain an argument about how successful government policies were in promoting economic growth in the USSR in the years 1918–28.

How successful were government policies in promoting economic growth in the USSR in the years 1918–28?

Key points:
- Heavy industry grew greatly due to the Five-Year Plans, but previous policies were less successful
- Agriculture rapidly grew during the NEP, but other polices were much less successful
- Light industry and consumer goods grew greatly during the NEP, but other polices were much less successful.

Introduction

Government policies were broadly successful in promoting the growth of heavy industry in the USSR in the years 1917–41. While Lenin's policies did not lead to great industrial growth, Stalin's successfully promoted the growth of heavy industry. Government policies were much less successful in promoting the growth of agriculture and light industry. While the NEP led to growth in both areas, War Communism and Stalin's economic policies led to either limited growth or decline in both areas.

Conclusion

In conclusion, government policies were successful in promoting the growth of heavy industry by 1941; however, there was much less success in agriculture and light industry.

The Stalin era: recovery from war after 1945

The Second World War devastated the Soviet economy. Using the techniques developed in the 1930s, economic planners set about rebuilding Soviet industry and reviving Soviet agriculture.

Soviet industry grew rapidly but agriculture grew more slowly. Consumer goods and housing remained in short supply as the government prioritised industrial reconstruction and rearmament over consumption or house building.

Economic consequences of the war

The Second World War set the Soviet economy back significantly. By 1945:
● 25 million people were homeless
● Soviet industry was producing around a third of what it had produced in 1940
● Soviet agriculture was producing around half the grain it had in 1940.

Industrial recovery

The post-war plans focused on heavy industry and rearmament. Almost 90 per cent of economic investment was devoted to developing heavy industry. By 1950 the Soviet economy was producing more coal, oil, electricity, iron and steel than it was in 1940. The economy was also the fastest growing in the world.

Military spending

The development of the **Cold War** meant that the Soviet Union continued to prioritise military spending. By 1952 the Soviet military budget was around 25 per cent of government spending.

Military spending led to real achievements. By 1949 Soviet scientists had successfully tested their first atomic bomb.

Economic problems

Between 1945 and 1953 the Soviet economy was plagued by problems.
● The economy remained inefficient because of the problems associated with the command economy.
● Soviet workers remained unproductive compared to the workers of other industrial nations.
● **Light industry** failed to grow. Less than 12 per cent of industrial investment in Stalin's last years went into light industry.
● Consumer goods remained scarce due to the lack of investment in light industry.
● High-tech production lagged behind other modern economies. High-tech production relies on the quality of the material and precision engineering, whereas the Soviet economy was designed to create vast quantities of material.
● Tractors, trucks and other high-tech goods were poorly made.
● Farming remained labour-intensive and a lack of incentives meant that productivity was low.

Stalin's economy

Stalin industrialised the Soviet Union. However, economic growth did not lead to a better standard of living for most citizens. Some historians argue that Stalin's economic policy reflected his gigantomania: a love of giant things. Stalin wanted to build giant factories, huge aeroplanes and produce vast quantities of steel. However, he was not interested in efficiency or in consumer goods. As a result, the economy industrialised in a way that served Stalin's gigantomania rather than the needs of the Soviet population.

Lenin and Stalin's 'achievement'

Communists who joined the Party during the 1930s believed that Stalin's economy was a huge achievement. From the 1930s Soviet Communists credited Lenin with laying the political foundation for Communism, and Stalin with establishing the world's first socialist economy. Later leaders would reform aspects of the system. However, the essentials of Lenin's one-party state and Stalin's command economy remained at the heart of the Soviet system until the late 1980s.

(i) Eliminate irrelevance   a

Below are a sample exam question and a paragraph written in answer to this question. Read the paragraph and identify parts of the paragraph that are not directly relevant to the question. Draw a line through the information that is irrelevant and justify your deletions in the margin.

> How successful were government policies in promoting economic development in the USSR in the years 1917–53?

As well as promoting economic development, government economic policies also played a role in promoting political stability. Lenin's Decree on Land won over the support of the peasants, which was crucial in the early phases of the revolution. Similarly, the NEP won back the support of the peasants in 1921. However, Communist economic policy was not wholly successful at promoting political stability. By 1921 War Communism had ruined farming to such an extent that there was famine and revolt in Tambov and Kronstadt. Similarly, collectivisation led to a revolt in the countryside. Rebellion against the government was particularly strong in Ukraine. Worse still, a government-created famine between 1932 and 1933 resulted in 5 million deaths. Stalin's industrial policy also created problems, for example the failure to invest in light industry meant that consumer goods were constantly in short supply. Moreover, Stalin did very little to help the 25 million people who were homeless following the war. Therefore, economic development only partially created political stability as the economy under Stalin never really addressed the needs of the people.

(i) Identify the concept   a

Below are five sample exam questions based on some of the following concepts:

- cause – questions concern the reasons for something, or why something happened
- consequence – questions concern the impact of an event, an action or a policy
- change/continuity – questions ask you to investigate the extent to which things changed or stayed the same
- similarity/difference – questions ask you to investigate the extent to which two events, actions or policies were similar
- significance – questions concern the importance of an event, an action or a policy.

Read each of the questions and work out which of the concepts they are based on.

1 How far do you agree that the introduction of the NEP in 1921 was the main turning point in Communist economic policy in the years 1917–53?

2 How successful was Communist economic policy in the years 1917–53? **AS**

3 To what extent did the aims of the Communist economic policy change in the years 1917–53?

4 How accurate is it to say that Stalin's policies thoroughly modernised the Soviet economy in the years 1928–53?

5 Was the failure of the NEP the main reason for Stalin's economic reforms of 1928–29? Explain your answer. **AS**

Changing economic priorities: agriculture

From Stalin's death to 1985 Soviet leaders remained convinced that Stalin's economic model would one day overtake capitalist economies.

Khrushchev's reforms led to further optimism. Between 1956 and 1958 the Soviet economy performed well. However, from 1959 growth slowed, and within a decade the economy was stagnant.

Investment in agriculture

Khrushchev recognised that collectivisation had led to an extremely inefficient agricultural sector. Therefore, he introduced important reforms in Soviet agriculture.

Incentives

Khrushchev paid farmers higher prices for their produce. This incentivised production and boosted farm incomes by 250 per cent between 1952 and 1956.

Virgin Lands Scheme

Khrushchev also wanted to increase the amount of land that was being farmed. Therefore, he launched the Virgin Lands Scheme, creating new farms in the northern Caucasus, Kazakhstan and Western Siberia.

Investment

Khrushchev tried to make farming more efficient through investing in:
- artificial fertilisers – boosting production by 40 per cent
- tractors – boosting production by 30 per cent.

Investment in agriculture grew from 3 per cent of the Soviet budget in 1954 to 12.8 per cent in 1959.

Agricultural successes, 1954–58

Khrushchev's policies were initially highly successful. Overall, agricultural production increased by around 35.3 percent from 1954–58. The early successes were so impressive that, in 1956, Khrushchev set a hugely ambitious target of overtaking US farm production by 1960.

Agricultural problems, 1954–64

In spite of initial success, there were still fundamental problems with Soviet agriculture.

Inefficiency

Soviet agriculture remained highly inefficient:
- The Virgin Lands Scheme required complex irrigation systems. This made the cost of production high.

- Agriculture was extremely labour-intensive. During the 1950s and 1960s around 50 per cent of the Soviet population worked in agriculture, compared to 5 per cent in the US. In spite of this, US agriculture produced double the amount of food produced by Soviet agriculture.

Slow growth

Between 1959 and 1964 agricultural growth slowed. During this period farm production grew by around 15 per cent. As a result, Soviet agriculture failed to meet Khrushchev's target of overtaking the USA in food production.

On-going problems

Poor performance was the result of significant economic problems.
- Central planning meant that farmers did not always use the correct fertiliser at the right time so it often went to waste.
- Khrushchev repeatedly reformed the ministries dealing with agriculture. Contradictory reforms led to administrative confusion.
- Soviet farms often had inadequate storage facilities, and therefore some of the food produced was wasted.
- Pay for agricultural workers increased, but remained inadequate.

Reform after Khrushchev

The failure of Khrushchev's reforms and the instability they created led leading Communists to reverse his reforms after 1964. What is more, Communist leaders rejected the very idea of reform after Khrushchev.

Agriculture, 1964–85

Brezhnev was content to manage the system that Stalin had set up. Brezhnev largely abandoned attempts to make agriculture more productive. Rather, he authorised large-scale grain imports from the West to keep food prices low.

High oil prices

Brezhnev was able to buy large amounts of grain from the West by selling oil. Oil prices were high during the 1970s, and therefore selling oil generated a great deal of income for the Soviet Union. Brezhnev used some of this to fund food imports.

ⓘ Establish criteria

Below is a sample exam question, which requires you to make a judgement. The key term in the question has been underlined. Defining the meaning of the key term can help you establish criteria that you can use to make a judgement.

Read the question, define the key term and then set out two or three criteria based on the key term, which you can use to reach and justify a judgement.

> How accurate is it to say that government policy failed to <u>modernise</u> Soviet agriculture in the years 1928 to 1964?

Definition

_____

_____

Criteria to judge the extent to which government policy failed to modernise Soviet agriculture in the years 1928 to 1964:

- _____

- _____

- _____

- _____

ⓧ Reach a judgement

Having defined the key term and established a series of criteria, you should now make a judgement. Consider how far the government policy failed to modernise Soviet agriculture according to each criterion. Summarise your judgements below:

- Criterion 1:

  _____

- Criterion 2:

  _____

- Criterion 3:

  _____

- Criterion 4:

  _____

Changing economic priorities: industry

Khrushchev wanted to modernise Soviet industry. He proposed investing in light industry in order to produce more consumer goods.

Khrushchev's reforms led to some economic modernisation. However, in the long term the Soviet economy went into decline.

Khrushchev's vision

Khrushchev wanted the Soviet Union to reach communism by 1980. Under communism, he believed that housing, transport and food would all be available freely.

Industrial problems

The Soviet Union faced three major problems, which hampered economic modernisation.
- Military spending: in the context of the Cold War **arms race** the Soviet Union was committed to high levels of military spending. Consequently, this limited the funds available for industrial investment.
- Command economy: Stalin's command economy was good at producing large quantities of basic goods such as steel and concrete. However, it was not designed to create complex or sophisticated goods such as cars or radios.
- Inefficiency: the command economy was highly inefficient; therefore it wasted resources which could otherwise have been used to modernise the economy.

The promotion of light industry

Khrushchev's Seven-Year Plan, launched in January 1959, increased investment in light industry. In so doing, it aimed to:
- increase production of consumer goods
- increase production of chemical fertilisers to support Khrushchev's agricultural policies, such as the Corn Campaign, an initiative to plant more corn.

Success of the plan

The plan boosted production of consumer goods and chemical fertilisers. However, the plan delivered lower growth than Khrushchev had expected:
- Production of consumer goods was 5 per cent below target
- Production of chemicals was around 20 per cent below target.

Ownership of cars, radios, refrigerators, washing machines and television sets increased.

However, by 1966 the Soviet Union still lagged behind other European nations. In terms of car ownership, for example, the Soviet Union was far behind:

Nation	Cars per 1,000
Soviet Union	5
United Kingdom	200
Holland	166
West Germany	207

Reasons for failure

The Seven-Year Plan under-performed for two main reasons:
- Khrushchev introduced contradictory reforms. In 1957 he decentralised economic planning. However, from 1958 to 1964 his reforms re-asserted central control.
- Khrushchev changed the targets of the plan in 1962, setting more ambitious goals.

Economic decline

Under Khrushchev growth rates slowed. This trend continued under Brezhnev. By 1980 economic growth had almost stopped. Economic decline came about for two main reasons.
- Refusal to change: after 1964 major economic reforms stopped. Therefore, long-term problems such as inefficiency and low productivity were never addressed.
- Brezhnev increased military investment, diverting resources away from economic growth.

The Soviet economy, 1964–85

Brezhnev abandoned Khrushchev's commitment to building Communism by 1980. However, he continued to promise a better standard of living. This was achieved by:
- Subsidising prices: the government kept the prices of consumer goods low. However, this led to shortages as demand for goods was higher than supply.
- A second economy: Brezhnev tolerated the growth of the black market or 'second economy'. This allowed Soviet citizens to buy consumer goods illegally.

Andropov's reform

Andropov attempted to address long-term problems in the Soviet economy through 'Operation Trawl'. KGB officials cracked down on drunkenness and absenteeism in an attempt to boost productivity. The campaign was short-lived and did not solve the underlying problems with the economy.

By 1985 the Soviet economy was stagnant. Successive leaders had failed to solve the problems of the command economy.

Eliminate irrelevance a

Below are a sample exam question and a paragraph written in answer to this question. Read the paragraph and identify parts of the paragraph that are not directly relevant to the question. Draw a line through the information that is irrelevant and justify your deletions in the margin.

> How accurate is it to say that the living standards of Soviet citizens improved dramatically in the years 1945–64?

In some areas, such as consumer goods, the living standards of Soviet citizens improved dramatically in the years 1945–64. Between 1928 and 1941 living standards had been low because of Stalin's Five-Year Plans, which included very few resources for creating consumer goods. This period was worse than the period under the NEP in which food tended to be plentiful. In 1945, after the Second World War, consumer goods were scarce. Stalin wanted to rebuild the Soviet Union's industrial economy, so consumer goods were not a priority. Also, Stalin wanted to re-arm because of the growing Cold War. However, after 1953 the government attempted to improve living standards. Khrushchev's Seven-Year Plan made consumer goods a priority and his Corn Campaign emphasised the need to produce more food. Neither was wholly successful, but the availability of consumer goods did improve, which meant that there was some improvement in living standards between 1945 and 64.

 Develop the detail

Below are a sample exam question and a paragraph written in answer to this question. The paragraph contains a limited amount of detail. Annotate the paragraph to add additional detail to the answer.

> How successful were government policies in promoting industrial development in the USSR in the years 1953–84?

Between 1953 and 1984 the Soviet government did not succeed in promoting light industry. Khrushchev's policies were aimed at promoting light industry. However, he had failed to improve light industry significantly. Brezhnev's policies were less radical, but he too wanted to increase the availability of consumer goods. Brezhnev also failed to improve light industry significantly. Overall, neither Brezhnev nor Khrushchev were able to promote light industry, because neither of them achieved the breakthrough that the Soviet economy needed.

Exam focus

Below is a sample high-level essay. Read it and the comments around it.

How accurate is it to say that Stalin's economic policies modernised the Soviet economy in the years 1928–53?

From 1928 to 1953 Stalin's economic policies transformed the Soviet economy from a relatively poor, largely agricultural economy to the fastest growing industrial economy in the world. However, modernisation implies more than industrialisation. Economic modernisation also means increasing productivity, increasing efficiency and producing high-tech goods. Stalin's policies clearly succeeded in industrialising the Soviet Union; however, the productivity remained a problem, and the Soviet economy was rarely efficient, and in most cases lagged behind other major economies in terms of technology. Therefore, while Stalin's policies transformed the Soviet economy, they did not wholly modernise it.

Stalin's economic policies clearly modernised the Soviet economy in the sense that by 1953 the Soviet economy had industrialised. In 1928 Soviet industry was still only a small part of the overall economy. Farming dominated the Soviet economy, with around 80 per cent of the workforce based on farms. Industrial output in 1928 was around the level that it had been in 1913. Stalin's Five-Year Plans transformed this. Between 1928 and 1941 industry grew at a phenomenal rate. Electricity output increased almost ten times, coal and steel production went up almost five times, and there was a three-fold increase in oil production. A great deal of this progress was destroyed during the Second World War, but the fourth and fifth Five-Year Plans rebuilt Soviet industry. Indeed, there was an 80 per cent rise in industrial output between 1945 and 1950 as a result of Stalin's policies. While this appears to be evidence that Stalin's policies modernised the Soviet economy, this judgement needs to be qualified. Stalin's policies led to the growth of heavy industry. Light industry did not grow as fast, and as a result industrialisation did not lead to an improvement of the standard of living of ordinary Russians. Less than 12 per cent of industrial investment in Stalin's last years went into light industry. Modernisation in Western economies led to the growth of light industry. Indeed, as the other economies grew, light industry became an increasing feature. Therefore, while Stalin's policies led to industrialisation they did not lead to modernisation in the full sense as light industry was never a major feature of the economy under Stalin.

Secondly, Stalin's economy was not truly modern because his policies never led to greater efficiency. Inefficiency was a constant feature of Stalin's economy. Collective farms were never fully mechanised. A lack of spare parts meant that many tractors could not be repaired, and therefore were never used to their full potential. Industrial production was often inefficient in the sense that it was wasteful. There was little co-ordination between the different branches of industry and before the late 1930s a lack of transport infrastructure meant that goods could not be transported easily around Russia, and therefore products often decayed in storage before they could be used. The economy was also inefficient because figures were falsified, which meant that planners were unable to develop plans based on reality.

Labour productivity, the rate at which workers produce goods, was also low in the Soviet Union. Agricultural workers were inefficient because they had no incentives to work hard as they did not own their land. On average, workers on private farms produced around 410 kilos of grain per hectare, whereas collective farms produced about 320 kilos per hectare. Clearly, Stalin's policies failed to modernise the economy in terms of efficiency and productivity. However, some of Stalin's policies did make the workforce more productive. In the late 1930s arriving late at work was criminalised. More effective still was the Stakhanovite movement.

The essay begins with a clear focus on the question and a valid definition of modernisation.

The contrast between economic growth and modernisation helps support the initial judgement.

The paragraph starts with a clear focus on one aspect of modernisation.

The paragraph covers the whole period mentioned in the question.

The essay recognises the problems with Stalin's model of industrialisation – in so doing, it deals with the complexities of Stalin's achievements, leading to a judgement that reflects the whole picture.

The paragraph concludes with a clear analytical link, reaching an interim judgement, supported by the criteria set out in the introduction.

The paragraph begins with a sustained focus on the question and the criteria set out in the introduction.

By providing incentives and allowing expert workers to organise their own production, the Stakhanovite movement increased labour productivity. Nonetheless, overall Stalin's policies tended to encourage inefficiency by failing to create incentives, and by allowing managers to falsify statistics. Consequently, Stalin's economic policies did not lead to true modernisation, because they tended to lead to inefficiency.

Finally, Stalin's economic policies did not modernise the Soviet Union, in the sense that they did not encourage the growth of high-tech industries. Stalin wanted higher production rates, but he was much less interested in quality and precision. High-tech production, however, relies on the quality of the material and the precision of the engineering. Consequently, while Stalin's policies led to massive production of raw materials they did not lead to the production of high-tech goods. The Soviet nuclear programme relied on very advanced production techniques, and allowed Stalin to produce an atomic bomb by 1949, only four years after the USA. However, the Soviet bomb project was exceptional; for the most part tractors, trucks, and other high-tech goods were poorly made. Therefore, the Soviet economy was not fully modernised because, with a few exceptions, Soviet industry was unable to deploy the most up-to-date techniques to make high-tech goods.

In conclusion, Stalin's economic policies clearly led to the growth of the Soviet economy, particularly Soviet industry. However, it is harder to conclude that his policies led to modernisation. Modernisation means more than industrial growth. Key features of modernisation were never achieved. The Soviet economy was never efficient, and the workforce, in spite of the Stakhanovite movement, never as productive as workers in the USA, Germany or Britain. Problems of inefficiency were particularly evident in Soviet agriculture, which was never fully mechanised, and therefore never truly modernised. Moreover, Soviet industry was never fully modernised in the sense that Stalin's plans did not allow light industry to develop, or high-tech industries to grow. Perhaps the best evidence that Stalin's economic policies failed to modernise the Soviet Union is the fact that Stalin's economic growth was 'self-consuming': inefficiency, low productivity and the uneven development of the economy meant that the Soviet Union failed to benefit from all of the economic growth that took place under Stalin, whereas in Western economies, which were more efficient and more balanced, economic growth made the nations richer.

The answer recognises that there were some improvements in terms of productivity. Therefore, it creates a balanced answer.

The conclusion reaches a fully substantiated judgement based on valid criteria.

This essay achieves a mark in Level 5 as it analyses a range of key issues relevant to the extent of modernisation. It also deploys sufficient knowledge to fully answer the question. It uses valid criteria to substantiate an overall judgement. Finally, the answer is logical, coherent and communicated with clarity and precision.

Key terms

One of the reasons that this essay is so successful is that it begins with a clear definition of the term in the question. Another example of an essay question involving a key term is below. Draw a plan for your answer to this question. Include a definition of the key term in your introduction and refer back to this definition in subsequent paragraphs.

How accurate is it to say that Khrushchev reformed the Soviet economy in the years 1956–64?

AS Level questions

How successful was Stalin's economic policy in the years 1928–53?

To what extent were Khrushchev's economic reforms successful in the years 1953–64?

3 Control of the people, 1917–85

State control of mass media and propaganda

REVISED

State control of the media and the use of propaganda were consistent features of Communist rule. Lenin wanted to free the working people of Russia from 'bourgeois ideas'. Therefore, he restricted press freedom. Despite some attempts to liberalise Communism under Khrushchev, censorship and propaganda remained essential features of Communist rule until 1985.

Lenin and the press

Lenin viewed the press and the media as central to advancing the revolution and ensuring the Communists retained power. Therefore, he introduced the following measures to establish government control:

- The Decree on the Press, established 1917, gave the government the power to close any newspapers that supported 'counter revolution'.
- The Revolutionary Tribunal of the Press, established 1918, gave the state the power to censor the Press. Journalists and editors who committed 'crimes against the people' could be punished by the Cheka (see page 42).
- The All-Russia Telegraph Agency (ROSTA), established 1918, gave the state control of all advertising and all news reporting.
- Glavlit, established in 1922, employed professional censors to examine all books, old and new, for anti-Communist ideas.

Initially, Lenin closed down papers that supported the Tsar or the **Provisional Government**. However, by mid-1918 he had outlawed opposition socialist papers as well. By 1921 the Communists had established control of the media throughout the Soviet Union.

Propaganda under Lenin

Propaganda under Lenin was often very experimental. Radical artists used new artistic techniques to spread the Communist message.

- Gustav Klutsis used **photomontage** to create posters advertising Lenin's electrification plan.
- El Lissitzky designed the poster 'Beat the whites with the red wedge', which used techniques from abstract art.
- ROSTA produced cartoon films to support the revolution.

Stalin's media

Censorship was tightened under Stalin. The works of Trotsky, Bukharin and Stalin's other rivals were banned. Additionally, Lenin's own works were 'edited' to remove complimentary statements about Stalin's opponents.

From 1928, Glavlit controlled access to economic data. Additionally, restrictions were placed on all kinds of 'bad news'. The Soviet media were forbidden from publishing stories about natural disasters, suicides, industrial accidents or even bad weather, in order to create the impression that the Soviet Union was a place in which only good things happened.

Propaganda focused on idealised images of workers and peasants happily building socialism in modern factories and farms.

Media under Khrushchev

Under Khrushchev, popular magazines were encouraged to publish readers' letters. This allowed Soviet citizens to express their own thoughts on 'non-political' subjects in magazines. Letters to women's magazines, like *Rabotnitsa* (the *Woman Worker*) exposed profound social problems. Readers complained about male alcoholism, inequalities in the home relating to childcare and housework and domestic violence.

Soviet propaganda changed too. Rather than presenting idealised images of workers and peasants, satirical cartoons were allowed. For example, *Krokodil*, a satirical magazine, poked fun at men who arrived at parades drunk, or late, or not at all.

Censorship was relaxed under Khrushchev during his cultural thaws (see page 48).

Media under Brezhnev

Brezhnev's media was very nostalgic. It focused on the victory of the Second World War in posters, books and films. However, Soviet cinema also made films set in contemporary Russia, which focused on fashionable citizens living in luxurious apartments. In so doing, they stoked public desire for consumer goods and fashion.

Khrushchev's cultural thaws were not repeated under Brezhnev. Nonetheless, rich Russians were exposed to Western ideas through Western magazines, which were available on the black market.

Mind map

Use the information on the opposite page to add detail to the mind map below.

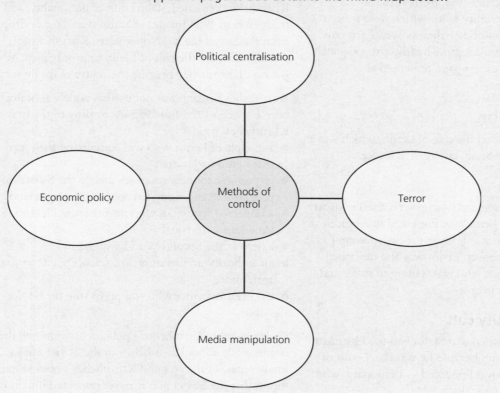

Political centralisation

Economic policy

Methods of control

Terror

Media manipulation

 Simple essay style

Below is a sample exam question. Use your own knowledge and the information on the opposite page to produce a plan for this question. Choose four general points, and provide three pieces of specific information to support each general point. Once you have planned your essay, write the introduction and conclusion for the essay. The introduction should list the points to be discussed in the essay. The conclusion should summarise the key points and justify which point was the most important.

How accurate is it to say that the principal reason for the survival of Communist rule in the Soviet Union in the years 1953–85 was Communist control of the media?

Soviet leaders were opposed to religion, but they understood its power. Therefore, from 1918 the government used personality cults, which were similar to religious cults, to consolidate their power. Each cult supported the Communist regime by inspiring personal loyalty to the leader. Leaders were presented as wise, humane and benevolent.

The cult of Stalin

The cult of Stalin built on the cult of Lenin, which was a decade old by the time Stalin emerged as leader.

The cult of Lenin

From 1918 Lenin's image and sayings were used regularly in Soviet propaganda. Lenin was presented in religious terms as a prophet who was leading the Soviet people to a better future. Moreover, Lenin was also described as being saintly, as a man who was willing to suffer and sacrifice his life for his people.

Stalin's personality cult

The Stalin cult emphasised that Stalin was the legitimate ruler of the Soviet Union because he was the 'Lenin of today'. Like Lenin, he was presented as a visionary, who was leading the way to socialism.

The Stalin cult required the manipulation of history in order to suggest that Lenin and Stalin had led the revolution together since 1917. From the early 1930s photographs were altered and histories were written stressing Stalin's leading role, as well as the treachery of former leaders such as Trotsky.

Stalin was presented as the '**vozhd**' the leader with ultimate authority. From 1941 Stalin was also presented as the 'Generalissimo', emphasising his role as the military leader who led the Soviet Union to victory in the Second World War.

Khrushchev's cult

Khrushchev criticised Stalin's cult of personality, and from 1955 to 1964 images of Stalin were largely dropped from the Soviet media. Nonetheless, Khrushchev continued to use the cult of Lenin in propaganda. What is more, Khrushchev became the centre of his own cult.

Khrushchev's image was not used as widely as Stalin's had been between 1928 and 1953. According to the new cult Khrushchev was:
- a disciple of Lenin who was completing the journey that Lenin had started
- responsible for new successes such as the Soviet space programme and rising harvests in the virgin lands
- a respected statesman who negotiated with the US President as an equal
- a hero of the Second World War
- an authority on literature, art, science, industry and agriculture
- the great reformer who was perfecting the Soviet system.

Problems with Khrushchev's policies undermined the claims made about Khrushchev in the Soviet media. The smaller scale of the cult and Khrushchev's obvious failures meant that the Soviet public never respected him as much as they respected Stalin and Lenin.

The cult of Brezhnev

A cult also developed around Brezhnev. Soviet propaganda under Brezhnev dropped references to Khrushchev, and rarely referred to Stalin. However, the Lenin cult persisted.

According to Soviet propaganda Brezhnev was:
- a great Leninist who continued Lenin's work
- a military hero who fought bravely in the Second World War
- dedicated to ensuring world peace through **detente**
- a true man of the people, who began his career in the steel industry.

The Brezhnev cult was counterproductive. Brezhnev was clearly a privileged bureaucrat not a great revolutionary. Therefore, Soviet citizens laughed at official claims that he was a hero. Whereas Stalin had been respected and feared, Brezhnev's cult led to ridicule.

Support or challenge?

Below is a sample exam question, which asks how far you agree with a specific statement. Below this is a series of general statements, which are relevant to the question. Using your own knowledge and the information on the opposite page decide whether these statements support or challenge the statement in the question and tick the appropriate box.

How far were personality cults the main reason for the stability of Soviet society in the years 1928–85?

	SUPPORT	CHALLENGE
The cults of Lenin and Stalin.		
The cults of Khrushchev and Brezhnev.		
The secret police.		
Economic policy.		
Media control.		

RAG – rate the timeline

Below are a sample exam question and a timeline. Read the question, study the timeline and, using three coloured pens, put a red, amber or green star next to the events to show:

- Red: events and policies that have no relevance to the question
- Amber: events and policies that have some significance to the question
- Green: events and policies that are directly relevant to the question.

How far were personality cults the main reason for the stability of Soviet society in the years 1918–64?

Now repeat the activity with the following questions:

1 How far was government's economic policy responsible for the stability of Soviet society in the years 1928–64?

2 How far did Soviet economic policy meet its aims in the years 1918–41?

3 How successful was Soviet economic policy in the years 1928–85? **AS**

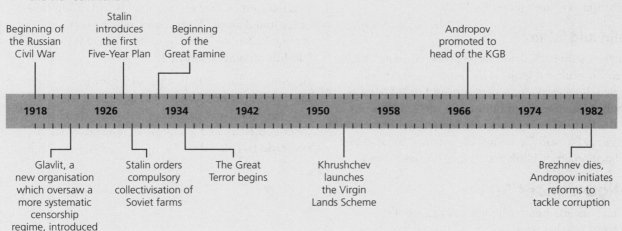

Attacks on religious beliefs and practices

Lenin believed that religion was an enemy of freedom and equality. Lenin also recognised that people who respected the teaching of the Church would never fully embrace Communist ideology. Therefore, Communist policies tended to persecute the Church. Nonetheless, the Communists were prepared to compromise with religious groups.

Religion under Lenin

Lenin introduced a series of decrees that defined the relationship of the government and religion:

- The 1917 Decree on Land gave peasants the right to seize land belonging to the Church.
- The 1918 Decree Concerning Separation of Church and State took away the traditional privileges of the **Orthodox Church**.

Lenin also used the Cheka to terrorise the Orthodox Church:

- In November 1917 Archpriest Ivan Kochurov was murdered outside Petrograd.
- In January 1918 Metropolitan Vladimir was tortured and shot in Kiev.
- Orthodox Priests in Moscow were massacred in January 1918 following a Church decree excommunicating the Bolsheviks.

The Living Church

In 1921 Lenin established the Living Church. It was established as a rival to the Orthodox Church. It removed the Church's traditional leaders and had a decentralised structure. Lenin hoped that these reforms would make it hard for the new Church to oppose the regime. However, the Living Church was not prepared to support the regime and the majority of Russians continued to believe in Christianity throughout the 1920s.

Lenin and Islam

Initially, Lenin backed attacks on property owned by Islamic institutions. However, this policy was quickly reversed. Rather, the new government funded Islamic schools. Moreover, Communists encouraged Muslims to join the Party. Communists were less antagonistic towards Islam than Russian Orthodox Christianity, because there had been no official link between Islam and Tsarism.

Religion under Stalin

Stalin's policies often had religious implications:

- Many churches were closed and turned into grain stores as a result of collectivisation.
- Stalin's terror destroyed Islamic groups. For example, Sufi groups in Turkestan were destroyed by 1936.

War and compromise

During the Second World War Stalin made a pragmatic alliance with the Church. Stalin asked Church leaders to support the government's war effort. In return, Stalin ended censorship of Church magazines, ended anti-religious propaganda and allowed some churches to re-open. Indeed, 414 churches re-opened during the Second World War.

Religion under Khrushchev

Khrushchev abandoned compromise, believing that religion had no place in a socialist society. Khrushchev's major anti-religious campaign started in 1958. It included:

- Closure of churches re-opened during and after the Second World War
- Anti-religious propaganda was reintroduced.
- placing Orthodox convents under surveillance.
- refusing believers access to holy sites.

Khrushchev also used the Soviet space programme to attack religion. Yuri Gagarin famously commented that having travelled up to the heavens he had found no God. Valentina Tereshkova, the first woman in space, also argued that her trip into space had led to the victory of atheism over 'the mysterious heavens that used to mystify the imagination'.

Religion, 1964–85

Brezhnev ended Khrushchev's anti-religious campaigns. He hoped that a scientific education would persuade young people that there was no God.

Under Brezhnev, the government started supporting anti-American Islamic groups in the Middle East. Therefore, Brezhnev established the Spiritual Board of Muslims of Central Asia and Kazakhstan, which allowed Soviet Islamic leaders and scholars to have limited contact with Muslims in other countries.

Brezhnev's shift in policy led to a shift in Communist ideology. Previous leaders had described Islam as a 'backward and barbarian' religion. Brezhnev described Islam as a 'progressive, **anticolonial** and revolutionary creed'.

Simple essay style

Below is a sample exam question. Use your own knowledge and the information on the opposite page to produce a plan for this question. Choose four general points, and provide three pieces of specific information to support each general point. Once you have planned your essay, write the introduction and conclusion for the essay. The introduction should list the points to be discussed in the essay. The conclusion should summarise the key points and justify which point was the most important.

To what extent was religion suppressed by Communist governments in the years 1918–85?

Eliminate irrelevance   a

Below are a sample exam question and a paragraph written in answer to this question. Read the paragraph and identify parts of the paragraph that are not directly relevant to the question. Draw a line through the information that is irrelevant and justify your deletions in the margin.

How far was government control over the lives of the people maintained in the years 1918–53?

There was extensive government control over the religious aspects of people's lives in the years 1918–53. Lenin argued that religion was an enemy of freedom. He also believed that people who respected the teaching of the Church would never fully embrace Communist ideology. Government control over religion was extended through terror. From 1918–53 terror was used extensively against the Orthodox Church. For example, Orthodox Priests in Moscow were massacred in January 1918 following a Church decree excommunicating the Bolsheviks. Stalin introduced big changes in policy such as the Five-Year Plans. But he continued to attack religious groups. For example, during collectivisation many Church buildings were closed and turned into grain stores. What is more, he destroyed Islamic groups such as Sufi groups in Turkestan. Nonetheless, not all religious activity was tightly controlled. Lenin's government funded Islamic schools, and Muslims were encouraged to join the Party during the 1920s. Similarly, Stalin ended censorship of Church magazines, and allowed some churches to re-open. Therefore, religion was tightly controlled, but control of religion was not complete because of the compromises made by the regime.

Attacks on opponents of the government

The Communist government's approach to opposition changed from 1917 to 1985. Moreover, the nature of opposition also changed during that time.

Control and opposition, 1917–28

Lenin introduced the Cheka in 1917 to target counter-revolutionaries. Initially, Lenin argued that the Cheka would be a short-term measure until the Communists had consolidated their power.

Lenin's definition of counter-revolutionary was extremely broad. Therefore, under Lenin the Cheka targeted:
● supporters of the former Tsar
● trade unions demanding higher pay for workers
● socialists who were in rival political parties.

Before 1921 the Cheka's activities included:
● requisitioning grain during the Civil War
● closing down opposition newspapers
● torturing and executing opponents of the regime, including people trading on the black market
● executing deserters from the Red Army.

During the NEP the Cheka attacked people they believed to be taking advantage of the freedom to trade. The Cheka viewed the following groups as 'class enemies':
● traders who became rich
● women who wore Western clothes and makeup
● young people who danced to Western music, such as jazz.

The Cheka also organised show trials of the former leaders of rival socialist parties.

The roles of Yagoda, Yezhov and Beria

Stalin's use of the Soviet secret police was significantly different from that of Lenin. Stalin used the secret police against the Party. Moreover, he used terror much more widely, sending millions to his gulags: forced labour camps. The secret police under Stalin were led by Yagoda, Yezhov and Beria.

Yagoda

Genrikh Yagoda became head of Stalin's secret police in 1934. Yagoda played an important role in the Great Terror: he collaborated with Stalin in turning the secret police against the Communist Party. However, under

Yagoda secret police officials tended to treat Communist officials with respect. As a result, the purge of Stalin's opponents occurred slowly under Yagoda. Therefore, Stalin was critical of Yagoda's leadership.

Yezhov

Yezhov was responsible for a massive escalation of the terror. Yezhov replaced Yagoda's agents with new officers who were willing to use torture much more widely. Yezhov was responsible for the worst years of the Great Terror, 1936–38.

The Great Terror became known as 'Yezhovshchina', meaning that the whole of Soviet society was engulfed in Yezhov's terror. During this period, around 1.5 million people, approximately 10 per cent of the male adult population, were arrested by the NKVD, the Soviet secret police; around 635,000 of these were deported and over 680,000 people were executed.

Show trials

The Moscow Show Trials were the most obvious sign of the Great Terror. Each trial removed the leaders of one of the Party's factions which had opposed Stalin in the 1920s.
● The Trial of the 16, organised by Yagoda in 1936, led to the execution of Zinoviev and his allies.
● The Trial of the 17, organised by Yezhov in 1937, led to the execution or imprisonment of Trotsky's main supporters.
● The Trial of the 21, organised by Beria in 1938, led to the execution of Bukharin and his former allies, including Yagoda.

The trials were designed to humiliate Stalin's opponents before punishing them.

Beria

Beria took over Stalin's secret police in 1938 as the Great Terror was winding down. During the Second World War, Beria organised mass deportations and mass executions of ethnic groups such as the Chechens, whom Stalin did not trust. After the war, Beria was put in charge of Soviet efforts to build a nuclear bomb. Beria was highly successful in this role, as the Soviet Union's first atomic bomb was tested successfully in 1949.

! Complete the paragraph

Below are a sample exam question and a paragraph written in answer to this question. The paragraph contains a point and specific examples, but lacks a concluding analytical link back to the question. Complete the paragraph, adding this link in the space provided.

> How far was government control over the lives of the people maintained in the years 1921–41?

The government maintained control of Soviet citizens to a considerable extent through the secret police. During the period of Yezhovshchina terror was widespread. Around 10 per cent of the population was executed or sent to a gulag during the Great Terror. This removed any potential opposition to Stalin by punishing his opponents and by striking fear into the hearts of those who escaped arrest by the NKVD. In the 1920s terror was less widespread, but the secret police still used the power to persecute priests, the Communists' political opponents and young people who pushed the boundaries of what was acceptable. Overall,

_____

_____

_____

i Developing an argument

Below are a sample exam question, a list of key points to be made in the essay, and a paragraph from the essay. Read the question, the plan and the sample paragraph. Rewrite the paragraph in order to develop an argument. Your paragraph should answer the question directly, and set out the evidence that supports your argument. Crucially, it should develop an argument by setting out a general answer to the question and reasons that support this.

> How accurate is it to say that mass political terror was a consistent feature of Soviet rule in the years 1918–53?

Key points:

- Mass political terror reached its height during the Great Terror.
- The Red Terror and Civil War were key features of the period of consolidation.
- Terror was still a feature of Soviet society during the NEP and in Stalin's last years.
- Terror during the NEP and Stalin's last years was more limited, although its impact extended beyond those directly targeted.

Mass political terror reached its height during the Great Terror. Between 1935 and 1938 Stalin's NKVD, first under the leadership of Yagoda, then under Yezhov and finally Beria, unleashed terror against government officials and Party members. The terror tended to impact men more than women — in fact only 5 per cent of Stalin's victims were female. The three Moscow Show Trials attacked some of the most senior members of the Party, and the NKVD's new conveyor belt system sped up the process so that millions of 'enemies of the people' could be tortured and forced to confess. The Great Terror claimed the lives of around 10 million victims — roughly 10 per cent of the Soviet population.

Khrushchev's policy of de-Stalinisation led to a scaling back of terror. However, Brezhnev was concerned about opposition to the regime. Therefore, he put a greater emphasis on controlling opponents. This approach continued until 1985. Nonetheless, there was no return to the mass terror of the Lenin and Stalin period.

Andropov's suppression of dissidents, 1967–82

Andropov, like Brezhnev, was a conservative and therefore suspicious of Khrushchev's liberalisation. Andropov rejected the use of mass terror, and preferred to minimise the use of violence. Rather, he wanted to use the Soviet secret police to target specific individuals – a tiny minority who refused to conform, who were known as dissidents.

Andropov's strategies

Andropov rejected show trials or other public attempts to control Soviet citizens, as he did not want to draw too much attention to the repressive side of the regime. Rather he:

- Allowed dissident artists to emigrate. Indeed, over 100,000 potential 'trouble makers' were allowed to leave the Soviet Union.
- Sent opponents of the regime to mental asylums, where they received 'treatment' for their 'paranoid reformist delusions'.
- Invested in surveillance and put pressure on those he believed might be dangerous to conform through a strategy of issuing formal warnings. Around 70,000 Soviet citizens received a secret police warning in the 1970s.
- Organised the demotion or sacking of dissidents. Indeed, many intellectuals ended up working as cleaners during the 1970s as a punishment for their anti-Soviet attitudes.
- Used intimidation tactics. For example, he sent bulldozers to destroy an illegal art exhibition in 1974. The exhibition became known as the 'Bulldozer Exhibition'.

Andropov's success

Andropov failed to stamp out opposition. Indeed, throughout the period networks of dissidents published illegal material. Homemade, self-published *samizdat* magazines contained literature and poetry that the Soviet authorities believed was counter-revolutionary.

Andropov was also forced to move cautiously against dissidents who were known in the West. Pressure from Western governments meant that dissidents like the physicist Andrei Sakharov, and the writer Aleksandr Solzhenitsyn remained free.

Popular discontent, 1982–85

Andropov became leader of the Soviet Union, but he continued to be head of the secret police. His policies were informed by secret reports on popular discontent. They indicated that Soviet citizens were:

- anxious about the slow improvement in living standards
- dissatisfied with the quality and availability of food and consumer goods
- resentful at the privileges and corruption of Party members.

Moreover, according to KGB reports, loss of faith in the system led to **social malaise**, which included an increase in:

- alcoholism
- poor labour discipline
- increased black market trade
- avoidance of military service
- demand for Western goods
- sympathy for strikes taking place in Poland
- increased Church attendance
- falling birth rate.

Dealing with discontent, 1982–85

Andropov introduced a series of polices designed to tackle the malaise.

- Anti-corruption: Andropov investigated senior Party officials, such as Brezhnev's Minister of the Interior Nikolai Shchelokov, who used Soviet resources to make themselves rich.
- Anti-alcohol campaign: workers could be sacked for drunkenness.
- Operation Trawl: an anti-drunkenness and anti-absenteeism campaign. KGB officers visited parks, restaurants and train stations arresting people who were drunk or who were absent from work.

Operation Trawl led to less absenteeism in the short term. However, Andropov became ill soon after his appointment as leader and was unable to sustain the campaigns.

Spectrum of importance

Below are a sample exam question and a list of general points, which could be used to answer the question. Use your own knowledge and the information on the opposite page to reach a judgement about the importance of these general points to the question posed. Write numbers on the spectrum below to indicate their relative importance. Having done this, write a brief justification of your placement, explaining why some of these factors are more important than others. The resulting diagram could form the basis of an essay plan.

How accurate is it to say that terror was the main method by which the Soviet government maintained control of the people in the years 1953–85?

1 Terror
2 The economic policy
3 Leadership cults
4 Censorship and media control

Least important   Most important

Turning assertion into argument

Below are a sample exam question and a series of assertions. Read the exam question and then add a justification to each of the assertions to turn it into an argument.

How far do you agree that the aims and methods of the Soviet secret police under Brezhnev were radically different from those of secret police under Stalin?

The aims of the secret police under Brezhnev were radically different from those of the secret police under Stalin in the sense that

However, there were some similarities between the aims of the secret police under Brezhnev and those under Stalin in the sense that

The methods of Brezhnev's secret police were radically different from Stalin's secret police in the sense that

However, there were some similarities between the methods of Brezhnev's secret police compared with Stalin's secret police in the sense that

The state and cultural change, 1917–53

Soviet leaders believed that art was a powerful tool for winning over the public. Between 1917 and 1953 Soviet art changed dramatically from radical avant-garde works to more traditional Socialist Realism.

Proletkult

Following the October Revolution some Communists tried to stimulate the growth of a truly proletarian form of art. Anatoly Lunacharsky, the new People's Commissar of Enlightenment, established Proletkult, the proletarian culture movement, to help nurture artistic talent among working people. By 1920 Proletkult set up 300 studios across Russia and published *Gorn* (Furnace), a monthly magazine that showcased the work of proletarian artists. Lunacharsky hoped that this would lead workers to make art reflecting their own experiences and the values of the new society.

Lenin and the end of Proletkult

Lenin was critical of Lunacharsky's philosophy and Proletkult. Lenin argued that the best culture was universal: it was neither bourgeois nor proletarian; rather it reflected the human spirit.

Lenin also had misgivings about Proletkult. He believed the work that was being produced was too avant-garde for working people to understand. What is more, Proletkult was independent of Party control, which worried Lenin.

In October 1920 Proletkult lost its independence and became part of the Commissariat of Education. Funds for radical projects were cut and money diverted to traditional arts such as ballet.

The avant-garde

The Revolution led to a new movement among painters, sculptors and film-makers. Inspired by the revolution, they experimented with new styles and techniques designed to generate a new, revolutionary art.

Avant-garde artists experimented with a variety of influences such as chance, geometric shapes, technology and the influence of dreams in order to create new kinds of art.

Avant-garde artists collaborated with the Communist government to produce propaganda:

- Vladimir Mayakovsky made simple graphic posters during the Civil War.
- Alexander Rodchenko is the most famous avant-garde photographer, who used techniques such as photomontage to make posters celebrating the revolution.
- Dziga Vertov, an experimental film-maker, used experimental techniques such as slow motion to produce a series of documentary films called Kino-Pravda (film-truth).

Socialist Realism

Stalin had strong views on art. He was suspicious of the avant-garde and experimental techniques. He argued that art should use traditional techniques to serve the government. In the early 1930s this approach became known as 'Socialist Realism'.

In painting, this came to mean art that was realistic, in the sense that pictures looked a lot like photographs, and socialist in the sense that they were paintings of factory construction or workers producing raw materials.

In terms of literature, the new style meant novels had to have a plot that ordinary people could follow, and had to focus on a subject that was related to building socialism. Fyodor Gladkov's 1924 novel *Cement* was held up as an example. The novel tells the story of a group of workers who, having played a major role in the Civil War, reconstruct a cement factory.

Lenin and Stalin also became the focus of paintings and other forms of art. Fedor Shurpin's *Morning of Our Motherland* (1949), for example, shows Stalin standing in a landscape transformed by collectivisation and industrialisation.

Soviet art, 1917–53

Between 1917 and 1953 Soviet art transformed from free, experimental and independent art to art that was dominated by government control and highly conservative in style.

Identify key terms a

Below is a sample Section A question, which includes a key word or term. Key terms are important because their meaning can be helpful in structuring your answer, developing an argument, and establishing criteria that will help form the basis of a judgement.

> How accurate is it to say that Communist policy towards the arts became increasingly repressive in the years 1918–53?

- First, identify the key word or term. This will be a word or phrase that is important to the meaning of the question. Underline the word or phrase.
- Secondly, define the key phrase. Your definition should set out the key features of the phrase or word that you are defining.
- Third, make an essay plan that reflects your definition.
- Finally, write a sentence answering the question that refers back to the definition.

Now repeat the task, and consider how the change in key terms affects the structure, argument and final judgement of your essay.

> How far do you agree that Soviet culture was transformed in the years 1918–53?

You're the examiner a

Below are a sample exam question and a paragraph written in answer to this question. Read the paragraph and the mark scheme provided on page 99. Decide which level you would award the paragraph. Write the level below, along with a justification for your choice.

> How far do you agree that Soviet culture was transformed in the years 1918–53?

Soviet culture was transformed in the years 1918–53 in the sense that it was became increasingly controlled by the government. Lunacharsky's initial vision was that all working people would be able to participate in making art. As People's Commissar of Enlightenment, he tried to make this vision a reality by setting up Proletkult, an independent organisation run by workers and artists. Proletkult ran 300 studios and published its own magazine, Gorn (Furnace). Lenin did not trust Proletkult, because it was independent of Party control. Therefore, in October 1920 Proletkult lost its independence and became part of the Commissariat of education. This was a genuine transformation in culture because the nature of artists' work changed from being free to being controlled by the state. Indeed, art remained dominated by the government for the rest of Lenin's rule and throughout Stalin's rule.

Level:

Mark:

Reason for choosing this level and this mark:

Khrushchev wanted to allow more cultural freedom. Indeed, as part of his programme of de-Stalinisation he initiated a series of cultural 'thaws' in which work that was critical of some aspects of government policy was tolerated. However, Khrushchev's policy was also characterised by freeze periods in which the government re-imposed tight control. Brezhnev was much more traditional, and therefore his government fought a continual battle with artists and others who refused to conform.

Thaw and nonconformity, 1954–64

Khrushchev wanted to forge an alliance between the Party and creative intellectuals. Therefore, he permitted more creative freedom in a series of thaws.

- 1953–54: following Stalin's death, the government allowed the publication of new works of literature, including Ilya Ehrenburg's *The Thaw*, which were critical of Stalin's terror.
- 1956–57: following Khrushchev's Secret Speech (see page 14), there was another period of cultural liberalisation. Works such as Vladimir Dudintsev's novel *Not by Bread Alone*, which was critical of Party bureaucracy under Stalin, were published.
- 1961–62: following the removal of Stalin's body from Red Square, a number of books were published that were critical of aspects of Stalin's rule. Aleksandr Solzhenitsyn's short story *One Day of Ivan Denisovich*, for example, tells of the life of a prisoner in the gulag.

However, during each thaw artists went further than the authorities would tolerate. For example, Boris Pasternak's novel *Doctor Zhivago* (1954) was critical of Leninism. Once artists began going too far Khrushchev re-imposed restrictions.

Nonconformity from the 1950s

While Khrushchev was prepared to tolerate some freedom of expression, he refused to accept widespread nonconformity. For Khrushchev, alcoholics and lazy government officials were examples of nonconformity that he wanted to challenge.

Khrushchev began a poster campaign encouraging citizens to challenge nonconformist behaviour. This policy was known as 'popular oversight', and was supported by posters created by graphic designers such as V. Fomichev and N. Denisovsky. For example, posters such as *The Lazy Bureaucrat* (1961) and *The Alcoholic* (1959) encouraged people to look out for nonconformist behaviour and to challenge it where it occurred.

Khrushchev was particularly critical of nonconformist women. He started an official campaign against 'stilyaga' (style hunters), young women who wore Western fashion. Khrushchev claimed that fashion was frivolous and wasteful. What is more, he assumed that fashionable clothes implied sexual promiscuity. As a result, there were official campaigns against Western fashion and 'loose women' in the late 1950s and early 1960s.

Clashes between artists and the government to 1985

Brezhnev abandoned cultural liberalisation. Indeed, in 1964 he authorised the trial of authors Andrei Sinyavsky and Yuli Daniel, who were arrested for producing 'anti-Soviet agitation and propaganda'. The Sinyavsky–Daniel Trial, which took place in 1966, was essentially a show trial. Both writers, who had risen to fame under Khrushchev, were sent to labour camps.

Dissident artists

Many artists produced work and took part in secret shows. For example:
- In 1968 artist Nonna Goriunova performed *Forest Ritual*, a piece of experimental theatre, (1968) in a wood.
- In the 1970s the Moscow Conceptualists published *samizdat* literature exposing the dullness of life under the Communists.
- The Mitki Collective put on secret shows in Leningrad exposing the hypocrisy of Communist officials. Dmitry 'Mitya' Shagin, the founder of the collective, encouraged his followers to demonstrate their rejection of the system by drinking cheap wine and wearing shabby clothes.

Some of these events were raided by the police; others carried on without official intervention. Nonetheless, the Soviet authorities remained suspicious of any group that championed freedom of expression.

Identify the concept

Below are five sample exam questions based on some of the following concepts:

- **cause** – questions concern the reasons for something, or why something happened
- **consequence** – questions concern the impact of an event, an action or a policy
- **change/continuity** – questions ask you to investigate the extent to which things changed or stayed the same
- **similarity/difference** – questions ask you to investigate the extent to which two events, actions or policies were similar
- **significance** – questions concern the importance of an event, an action or a policy.

Read each of the questions and work out which of the concepts they are based on.

1 To what extent were the cultural developments of the 1920s suppressed by Stalin's regime?

2 How far did government policy towards arts and culture change in the years 1953–85? **AS**

3 To what extent did the Soviet secret police deal successfully with opposition in the years 1918–53? **AS**

4 To what extent did the fundamental features of Stalin's government remain in place in the period 1953–85?

5 How successful were government cultural policies in promoting political stability in the USSR in the years 1928–64?

You're the examiner

Below are a sample exam question and a paragraph written in answer to this question. Read the paragraph and the mark scheme provided on page 99. Decide which level you would award the paragraph. Write the level below, along with a justification for your choice.

How accurate is it to say that, in the years 1953–89, the government of the Soviet Union became increasingly stable?

Brezhnev's government abandoned reform and sought to create stability. However, Brezhnev's policies led to stagnation which, in the long run, undermined the stability of the Soviet government. Brezhnev's policy of the 'stability of the cadres' helped create stability in the period 1965–1970 as it won back the support of Party members for the leadership. However, over time it led to the creation of a gerontocracy in which leaders were increasingly unable to govern effectively because of their age. This undermined the stability of Communist rule as it led to increasing criticism of the leadership. Additionally, Brezhnev's cultural policies created stability in the short term. The Sinyavsky–Daniel trial signalled an end to cultural thaws, which had destabilised Communist rule under Khrushchev. However, in the long term, cultural conformity led to the emergence of a dissident movement that undermined government. Clearly, Brezhnev's government's decision to abandon reform led to the establishment of a stable government, but stagnation increasingly destabilised the government as the problems with Communism became more apparent.

Level:

Mark:

Reason for choosing this level and this mark:

Exam focus

Below is a sample high-level essay. Read it and the comments around it.

How accurate is it to say that Stalin's death was the main turning point in Soviet art and culture in the years 1918–1985?

There were a number of important turning points in Soviet art and culture in the years 1928–1985. Stalin's death was the main turning point. Nonetheless, there were others including the abolition of Proletkult, and the Sinyavsky–Daniel Trial of 1966.

First, Stalin's death was undoubtedly a turning point in Soviet art. Stalin's death led to a process of de-Stalinisation. In art and culture this meant a degree of freedom to criticise the government. This was clear during the 'thaws' of 1953–54, 1956–67 and 1961–62. During these cultural thaws, work critical of Stalin's terror was published including Ilya Ehrenburg's *The Thaw*, and Aleksandr Solzhenitsyn's short story *One Day of Ivan Denisovich*. Work was also published that was critical of other aspects of the regime such as Vladimir Dudintsev's *Not by Bread Alone*, which was critical of Party bureaucracy under Stalin. Also Khrushchev encouraged cartoons that criticised other parts of Soviet government such as *The Lazy Bureaucrat* (1961) and *The Alcoholic* (1959), which pointed out problems with the USSR. However, the change was not complete, as there were still limits to artistic expression. For example, Boris Pasternak's novel *Doctor Zhivago* (1954) was banned as it was critical of Lenin. Moreover, at the end of each 'thaw' there was a cultural freeze, which indicates that Stalin's death did not transform Soviet culture as there was not permanent change.

The Sinyavsky–Daniel Trial of 1966 was a more significant turning point, because it showed that the thaws were permanently over. Brezhnev's policy was much more conservative than Khrushchev's. Under Brezhnev, Andrei Sinyavsky and Yuli Daniel were arrested for producing 'anti-Soviet agitation and propaganda'. Their 1966 trial was essentially a show trial and they were both found guilty and sent to labour camps. After the trial, there were no more thaws. Indeed, the trial was a major change as Sinyavsky and Daniel had been allowed considerable freedom and become famous under Khrushchev. Following the trial, dissident artists such as Nonna Goriunova and the early 1980s Mitki Collective were persecuted consistently. Therefore, the Sinyavsky–Daniel Trial was a more significant turning point than Stalin's death as Stalin's death led to short-term thaws, whereas the Sinyavsky–Daniel Trial led to a long-term freeze.

Finally, the abolition of Proletkult was the most significant turning point in the history of Soviet art and culture from 1918–1985 because it abolished artistic independence. Proletkult embodied the ideals of Anatoly Lunacharsky, the first People's Commissar of Enlightenment. Lunacharsky wanted all working people to have the opportunity to make art. Therefore, he established Proletkult, which set up 300 studios across Russia and published a monthly magazine known as *Gorn* (Furnace). However, Lenin was suspicious of Proletkult as it was independent of the government and therefore could express anti-government views. Under pressure from Lenin, Proletkult became part of the government in 1920, merging with the Commissariat of education. This was the most significant turning point as from 1920 onwards, with the exception of the three short-lived thaws, the government controlled all artistic work. In this way, it is the most significant turning point as it had the longest term consequences. Additionally, it was significant because it allowed the government to impose its own style on Soviet artists. Once Proletkult became part of the government, funding for workers' art was cut, and the government began funding traditional forms of art. This continued into the 1930s when Socialist Realism became the official style for paintings and

---

The essay begins with a clear focus on the question. It focuses effectively on change as it considers a number of possible turning points from across the period 1966–85.

The paragraph opens by considering the ways in which Stalin's death led to change. It gives well-selected examples of artistic change.

The paragraph is balanced as it recognises evidence that the change was not complete.

The judgement is based on the criteria of the permanence of change.

This paragraph covers the later part of the chronology, going right up to the early 1980s.

The judgement is based on the same criteria as the analysis of the previous turning point.

This paragraph covers the initial part of the chronology. In so doing, the essay covers the whole period 1918–85.

novels, and avant-garde work was suppressed. Again, this was an important turning point as after Proletkult lost its independence art in the Soviet Union became much more traditional, and again, this continued to be the case until 1985.

In conclusion, Stalin's death was a turning point for Soviet art and culture, as it allowed some brief cultural thaws. However, the thaws were not deep, as artistic work was still banned, and it was not long-lasting, as the thaws stopped in 1962 and the freeze lasted until 1985. The Sinyavsky–Daniel Trial was more significant as its consequences were more long-lasting. However, Proletkult's loss of independence was the most important turning point as it led to state control of art from that point on, with the exception of the brief thaws, and it led to a more conservative form of art ending the experimentation of the avant-garde.

Again, the judgement is based on the same criteria.

The conclusion summarises the argument and reaches a supported overall judgement based on valid criteria.

This essay achieves a mark in Level 5 as it analyses a range of possible turning points, and reaches a supported overall judgement regarding which was the most significant. It maintains a consistent focus on the question, covers the whole chronology and uses valid criteria to support its judgement. The answer is coherent and communicated with precision.

> **Linking factors**
>
> One of the reasons why this essay is so successful is that it draws links between the factors it discusses. Read through the essay again, and highlight the points at which the factors are linked. Below are more examples of exam questions. Draw plans for your answers to these questions. Annotate your own plans to show how you would link the different factors discussed in the essays.

AS Level questions

Was the use of terror the main reason for the survival of the Communist regime in the Soviet Union in the years 1964–82? Explain your answer.

In the period 1953–64, was the main consequence of de-Stalinisation the ending of mass terror? Explain your answer.

To what extent were there changes in Soviet culture in the years 1918–53?

To what extent had the Communist Party established control over the Soviet Union in the first decade of Communist rule?

How significant was state control of mass media in the growth of Communist power in the years 1918–28?

4 Social developments, 1917–85

Social security, 1917–53

One goal of Soviet economic policy was to distribute wealth fairly to all workers and peasants. However, this commitment to a decent job, good housing and other social benefits tended to be secondary to other economic priorities.

Full employment and social benefits

Lenin and Stalin were committed to the principle that all able-bodied adults should work.

War Communism

Under War Communism, work became compulsory. This meant that all Soviet citizens between the ages of 16 and 50 had to either work or fight. In return, they received a work card, which entitled them to a variety of social benefits. Food and fuel was rationed by *Prodraspred* (Section of General Distribution). Additionally, other amenities such as housing and transport were provided free to urban workers. Laundries and crèches were also provided in cities.

In practice, War Communism failed. Rations were insufficient for workers' needs, and by 1920 workers were beginning to abandon factories in search of food in rural areas. Indeed, the urban population fell by 25 per cent during the Civil War.

The NEP

During the NEP the economy changed. Unemployment returned as soldiers were demobilised, and workers were sacked to make industry more efficient. Free crèches were also abolished making it harder for women to work. By 1924, 18 per cent of the urban workforce was unemployed.

Nonetheless, during the 1920s the Soviet Union developed the most comprehensive system of social benefits in the world. Urban workers were entitled to:

- social insurance, which paid disability benefits, maternity benefits, unemployment benefits and medical benefits
- the government invested in education for urban workers and their families.

This system was administered by trade unions and covered 9 million urban workers during the 1920s. However, the peasants had no right to this welfare.

Work and benefits under Stalin

Compulsory work was reintroduced under Stalin. The introduction of the Five-Year Plans led to full employment for male urban workers and jobs for an increasing number of women (see page 56). Labour discipline in Stalin's factories was harsh, and conditions were often dirty and dangerous. While standards of living improved slowly at best, a system of social benefits emerged. It included: food rations, access to better transportation due to the construction of the Metro and over 30,000 km of railways, and vaccines for common diseases such as typhus and malaria were made universally available from 1947. Factory canteens provided meals for workers.

Problems with welfare

There were problems with the system that developed under Stalin.

- Peasants benefited much less than workers. For example, they were not entitled to rations.
- Food was a major problem. In order to make up for shortages, work canteens used rotten food, animal feed and other products that were unfit for human consumption, which led to illness.
- Sanitation in factories and farms was often inadequate, leading to lice infestations and outbreaks of dysentery and vomiting.

Housing

Housing was a continual problem in the period 1917–53.

- In the 1920s, Soviet authorities redistributed existing housing, taking it away from rich property owners and allowing poor people to live in the houses of the capitalists and aristocrats.
- Experiments in architecture such as the Narkomfin Apartment House in Moscow provided excellent housing. However, these projects were rare as they were expensive.
- Under Stalin existing urban housing was divided into *kommunalka* – communal apartments. Entire families would live in a single room of between 4 and 5.5 square metres. In some cases, whole families lived in under-stairs cupboards or corridors.
- Barracks-style dormitories were constructed to house factory workers in new factory towns such as Magnitogorsk. In the Moscow Coal Fields dormitories contained only 15,000 beds for the 26,000 workers.

Spot the mistake a

Below are a sample exam question and a paragraph written in answer to this question. Why does this paragraph not get into Level 4? Once you have identified the mistake, rewrite the paragraph so that it displays the qualities of Level 4. The mark scheme on page 99 will help you.

> How accurate is it to say that there was a very significant difference in the social and economic policies of Lenin's and Stalin's governments in the years 1918–53?

In some ways social policies were quite similar under Lenin and Stalin. In the early 1920s Lenin constructed a comprehensive system of social benefits for urban workers. Similarly, workers under Stalin were entitled to a large range of benefits. Another similarity was the treatment of peasants. Under Lenin and Stalin peasants did not receive the kinds of benefits that workers were entitled to. In this way, there were clearly some similarities between the social policies of Lenin and Stalin because in both cases workers received a much better standard of social security than peasants.

Complete the paragraph

Below are a sample exam question and a paragraph written in answer to this question. The paragraph contains a point and specific examples, but lacks a concluding analytical link back to the question. Complete the paragraph adding this link in the space provided.

> How far do you agree with the opinion that there was a steady improvement in the lives of Russian peasants over the years 1918–53?

There was little in the way of steady improvement in the lives of Russian peasants over the years 1918–31. First, there were many policies that made the lives of peasants worse in the period. War Communism relied on grain requisitioning, which meant the peasants were not paid for their produce or their labour. War Communism led to a famine, which killed 6 million Russian peasants. The NEP improved the lives of Russian peasants, however, peasants; lives were worse than those of workers as, unlike workers, they had no access to social insurance. Finally, the NEP was short-lived and collectivisation, again, led to millions of deaths, and the loss of land for peasants. Therefore, in the period 1918–31

_____

_____

Khrushchev, Brezhnev and the promotion of a stable society, 1953–85

Khrushchev and Brezhnev wanted to build on Stalin's achievements by improving welfare. Indeed, for Brezhnev these improvements were essential to a 'social contract', which underpinned his regime.

Welfare under Khrushchev

For Khrushchev, improving the lives of working people was a central part of his vision of socialism. Therefore:

- He doubled spending on healthcare from 1950 to 1959.
- He quadrupled the pensions budget from 1950 to 1965.
- In 1961 he introduced free lunches in schools, offices and factories, free public transport, and free pensions and healthcare for farmers.

As a result of Khrushchev's increased investment in welfare there were significant improvements in Soviet life expectancy:

	1950	1965
Death rate (per thousand of the population)	9.7	7.3
Infant mortality rate (per 1,000 live births)	81	27

Housing, 1953–85

Housing was one of Khrushchev's main priorities. His approach to housing was continued under Brezhnev. Khrushchev invested in the development of new building methods in order to solve the Soviet housing crisis. The result was the K-7 housing block nicknamed *Khrushchyovka*. These low-cost blocks could be constructed quickly and easily from large **prefabricated** concrete panels and standardised windows and doors, rather than being built slowly from brick. The new blocks allowed families to have an entire apartment, with running water and central heating, rather than being forced to live in a single room, or to share a dormitory.

Although they were designed as temporary buildings, *Khrushchyovka* became the standard model for all new homes. Construction of *Khrushchyovka* continued throughout the 1970s and 1980s.

Brezhnev's 'social contract'

Brezhnev abandoned Khrushchev's goal of achieving Communism by 1980 (see page 32). However, he continued to invest in welfare. Brezhnev viewed welfare provision as part of a 'social contract' between the government and the people. The 'social contract' was a **tacit** bargain in which the people supported the government and the government guaranteed a rising standard of living. Soviet citizens were guaranteed:

- job security, through guaranteed full employment
- low prices for essential goods
- a thriving second economy, free of government interference
- social benefits such as free healthcare
- some social mobility.

Brezhnev extended welfare provision, so that it included:

- subsidised rent
- subsidised electricity and water – most utilities were provided almost free of charge
- subsidised holidays
- increasing spending on healthcare and pensions every year.

Social stability

Generally, Brezhnev's 'social contract' succeeded in promoting social stability. During the late 1960s and 1970s Soviet citizens, particularly those in the cities, enjoyed the highest standard of living ever experienced in the Soviet Union. Through a combination of government benefits, and trading on the black market, most citizens were guaranteed a secure and comfortable life. At the same time, organised opposition to the government was extremely rare. Therefore, by ensuring a relatively high and rising standard of living Brezhnev's policies broadly succeeded in creating a stable society in the period 1964 to 1985.

Social problems

In spite of the increased welfare provision, social problems persisted under Brezhnev.

- Brezhnev's policies were based on very traditional ideas about the role of women. Women were often refused jobs in industry due to prejudice. Therefore, in some areas female unemployment was as high as 10 per cent.
- Life expectancy declined from 68 to 64 years for men during the 1970s. Alcoholism was one of the main causes.

! Delete as applicable

Below are a sample exam question and an introduction written in answer to this question. Read the introduction and decide which of the possible options (in bold) is most appropriate. Delete the least appropriate options and complete the paragraph by justifying your selection.

How significant was Soviet social policy in the promotion of a stable society in the period 1964–85?

Soviet social policy was **highly/moderately/barely significant** in the promotion of a stable society in the period 1953–85. Under Brezhnev Soviet social policy was part of the 'social contract' which was the government's main approach to ensuring stability. However, Andropov was actively suppressing dissidents during this period, and the Soviet media also played a significant role in promoting stability. Therefore, Soviet social policy was **highly/moderately/barely** significant in the promotion of a stable society in the period 1953–85 because

_____

_____

! Support or challenge?

Below is a sample exam question, which asks how far you agree with a specific statement. Below this is a series of general statements, which are relevant to the question. Using your own knowledge and the information on the opposite page decide whether these statements support or challenge the statement in the question and tick the appropriate box.

How far do you agree that the standard of living of all Soviet citizens improved in the years 1953–85?

	SUPPORT	CHALLENGE
Khrushchev and Brezhnev constructed *Khrushchyovkas*.		
Khrushchev's Virgin Lands Scheme increased agricultural production.		
Brezhnev's 'social contract' guaranteed job security.		
Brezhnev's 'social contract' guaranteed low prices.		
Under Brezhnev the Soviet economy stagnated.		
Khrushchev invested in healthcare and pensions.		
Inequalities between the country and the city remained.		

The changing status of women

The Communist Party was officially committed to creating a truly equal society. However, inequalities between men and women persisted. The status of women differed in the country and the city and the experience of women changed over time.

The status of women in Soviet towns

Women's status in Soviet towns changed over time.

Civil War

Immediately after the revolution Lenin set up *Zhenotdel* – the women's department of the Communist Party. Alexandra Kollontai, head of the *Zhenotdel*, believed that there were innate differences between men and women; therefore during the Civil War the *Zhenotdel* recruited women to work in crèches and orphanages where they could fulfil their 'natural nurturing role'. Some women also worked in factories due to labour shortages.

NEP

During the NEP, crèches were closed and those women who had worked in industry were sacked in order to free up jobs for men. Due to widespread unemployment and very limited government benefits many women were forced to work as prostitutes in the 1920s. It is estimated that 39 per cent of urban men used prostitutes in the 1920s.

Stalin's industry

Women joined the industrial labour force in large numbers due to the demands of the Five-Year Plans. Over 10 million women joined the labour force by 1940, increasing the female labour force by more than 300 per cent. During the Second World War women made up 75 per cent of the urban labour force. However:

- Women were only paid around 60–65% of men's wages.
- They were subjected to verbal and physical abuse in factories.
- Women tended not to get promotions.

Women workers, 1953–85

During the 1960s, around 45 per cent of industrial jobs went to women. However, women tended to be restricted to:

- production line work in light industry, which was intensive, but required low levels of skill, such as textile production
- heavy manual labour, which was also low-skilled.

During the 1960s another form of employment open to women was clerical or administrative work. Indeed, in the mid-1960s, 74 per cent of people employed in clerical positions in health services and education were women.

By the 1970s women dominated certain professions. By 1985 women made up:

- 70 per cent of medical doctors
- 75 per cent of employees in universities
- 65 per cent of people employed in art and culture.

Significantly, pay scales in these 'feminised' industries were lower than in male-dominated factory management.

The status of women in the countryside

During the 1920s, 1930s and 1940s a high proportion of women worked in agriculture. Women in the countryside performed a 'triple shift'. They provided agricultural labour on farms, they were responsible for household chores, and they were often engaged in handicrafts to supplement the family income.

Khrushchev wanted to recruit women to work on the Virgin Lands Scheme (see page 30). The campaign to recruit women focused on specific roles: women were required to act as milkmaids, gardeners, and to start families. Women were not recruited to work with machinery or drive tractors; rather the emphasis was on women as manual labourers and carers. Women in the Virgin Lands Scheme tended to do the lowest-paid and most demanding jobs. For example, of the 6,400 women recruited in August 1958 fewer than 450 found work in well-paid professional jobs.

Women continued to work in low-status, low-paid jobs in farming in the 1970s and 1980s. By 1970, 72 per cent of the lowest-paid Soviet farmers were women.

Professional opportunities also reflected the general prejudice that women played a nurturing role rather than a leadership role. Indeed, by 1980, 80 per cent of teachers in rural schools were women, whereas only 2 per cent of farm managers were women.

Simple essay style

Below is a sample exam question. Use your own knowledge and the information on the opposite page to produce a plan for this question. Choose four general points, and provide three pieces of specific information to support each general point. Once you have planned your essay, write the introduction and conclusion for the essay. The introduction should list the points to be discussed in the essay. The conclusion should summarise the key points and justify which point was the most important.

> To what extent was there a genuine improvement in the position of women in the Soviet Union in the years 1918–64?

Identify key terms   a

Below is a sample Section A question, which includes a key word or term. Key terms are important because their meaning can be helpful in structuring your answer, developing an argument, and establishing criteria that will help form the basis of a judgement.

> How far do you agree that in the years 1918–53 Soviet women made substantial gains in their position and status?

- First, identify the key word or term. This will be a word or phrase that is important to the meaning of the question. Underline the word or phrase.
- Secondly, define the key phrase. Your definition should set out the key features of the phrase or word that you are defining.
- Third, make an essay plan that reflects your definition.
- Finally, write a sentence answering the question that refers back to the definition.

Now repeat the task using the question below, and consider how the change in key terms affects the structure, argument and final judgement of your essay.

> How accurate is it to say that women in the Soviet Union experienced only limited changes in their employment opportunities in the years 1953–85?

The family

Communist views on the family and policies towards the family changed over time. Some Soviet leaders were determined to reform the family, while others were more conservative.

The family, 1917–35

Lenin's government was divided over the family. Alexandra Kollontai wanted to replace traditional family life with communal living and **free love**. Experiments in communal living took place, but they were abandoned by the mid-1920s.

Lenin, however, was more conservative. He was particularly critical of free love. Nonetheless, Lenin recognised the abuses that went on in traditional marriage, and therefore supported reforms proposed by *Zhenotdel* including:

- abortion on demand
- contraception
- easily accessible divorce
- legalisation of prostitution
- legalisation of male homosexuality (lesbianism had never been criminalised).

The relaxation of divorce laws led to rising divorce rates. Some men abused the system by marrying women and divorcing them once they became pregnant.

The Great Retreat, 1936–53

Under Stalin, Soviet family policy became much more conservative. Trotsky, writing in exile, contrasted the 'advances' made in family policies in the 1920s with what he called the 'Great Retreat' under Stalin.

Stalin's key aims were to increase birth rates, and cut divorce rates. He wanted to create stable families to serve the goal of economic development. To achieve this:

- Abortion was criminalised, unless the life of the pregnant woman was in danger.
- Contraception was banned.
- Male homosexuality was criminalised; consensual sex between men was punishable by 5 years in a labour camp.
- Lesbianism was treated as a 'disease'; lesbian women could be subjected to hypnotherapy in an attempt to 'cure' them.
- Sex outside of marriage was stigmatised.
- Divorce was made expensive and difficult to obtain; a first divorce cost approximately one week's wages, while subsequent divorces were more expensive.
- Following divorce, fathers were required to pay a minimum of one-third of their income to their former wives to support their children.

Stalin also adopted **pronatalist** policies offering financial incentives for women to have children.

- Women with seven children received 2,000 roubles a year for five years.
- This figure increased to 5,000 roubles for mothers with 11 children.

The family, 1953–64

Khrushchev introduced policies to liberate women. However, many of his policies were based on traditional assumptions. Khrushchev's family policies:

- legalised abortion in 1955
- increased paid maternity leave from 77 days to 112 days in 1956
- expanded crèche, child care facilities and communal laundries during the sixth Five-Year Plan
- introduced convenience foods, and mass produced clothing during the Seven Year Plan, in an attempt to end the 'double shift'
- aimed to make refrigerators widely available, ending the need for daily shopping trips.

In spite of these changes problems remained.

- Contraception remained hard to acquire.
- Crèches tended to open late and closed early, so that women were still unable to work full days.
- Domestic appliances were either less helpful than anticipated or less widely available.

The family, 1964–85

Family policy changed in 1965 with a new law that liberalised divorce. By 1979 around one-third of Soviet marriages ended in divorce.

Brezhnev's main aim for family policy was to increase the birth rate. Brezhnev's pronatal campaign emphasised 'natural differences' between the sexes, stressing women's 'natural' ability to nurture and 'natural' need for a strong man. By the late 1970s this pronatalist message was coupled with official criticism of women who 'neglected' their children by going to work. According to Brezhnev's propaganda, working women were responsible for juvenile delinquency, rising crime, drug taking, alcoholism and family break-up. This view persisted into the 1980s, and was reaffirmed by the last three Soviet leaders.

Eliminate irrelevance

Below are a sample exam question and a paragraph written in answer to this question. Read the paragraph and identify parts of the paragraph that are not directly relevant to the question. Draw a line through the information that is irrelevant and justify your deletions.

How accurate is it to say that there were major changes in the Communist family policy in the years 1918–85?

Divorce was one area where there were major changes in Communist family policy. In the early years Alexandra Kollontai advocated free love and introduced experiments in communal living. Lenin was also critical of traditional marriage and therefore he introduced easily accessible divorce. This changed radically under Stalin. During the 'Great Retreat' of the 1930s divorce was made much more difficult. Divorce became an expensive process, costing at least one week's wages. Moreover, divorced fathers were required to pay at least one-third of their income to their former wives to support their children. Stalin also banned contraception, although there were more employment opportunities for women under the Five-Year Plans. New divorce laws introduced in 1965 made divorce easier to obtain. Consequently, by 1979 around a third of marriages ended in divorce. Therefore, Soviet divorce policy changed significantly because there were reforms in the 1930s and again in the 1960s, which changed government policy towards divorce dramatically.

Identify an argument

Below are a sample exam question and two sample conclusions. One of the conclusions achieves a high mark because it contains an argument (an assertion justified by a reason). The other achieves a lower mark because it contains only description (a detailed account) and assertion (a statement of fact or an opinion, which is not supported by a reason). Identify which is which. The mark scheme on page 99 will help you.

To what extent was there a genuine improvement in the position of women in the Soviet Union in the years 1953–85?

Overall, there is clearly some evidence that the position of women in the Soviet Union improved in the years 1953–85. First, there was better housing and better healthcare, which improved the lives of women. Also education improved, and this also helped women. There were some important women who were role models such as Valentina Tereshkova who became the first woman in space in 1963. However, at the same time, there were propaganda campaigns that blamed women for the problems of Soviet society, through neglect. Also there were pronatal campaigns that tried to ensure that women fulfilled their 'natural' role as mothers. Clearly, there were improvements, but not in all areas.

In conclusion, the lives of all citizens improved in the period 1953–85, in the sense that living standards, healthcare and education improved. However, the position of women in the Soviet Union did not improve because they were deliberately denied important opportunities and key privileges were reserved for men. Women did gain more working opportunities; however, their position remained the same because female employment tended to be in clerical roles, agricultural jobs or light industry, and therefore they were less well paid and more junior than men. Equally, government policies such as the production of consumer goods under Khrushchev and the pronatal campaign under Brezhnev re-emphasised women's subordinate position in the home. There were some improvements such as the legalisation of abortion and growing representation of women in the soviets, but these only had a limited impact on work and politics. In this sense, the position of women did not improve greatly because Soviet policy tended to emphasise women's traditional position as wife and mother and to protect the dominant position of men within the economy and government.

Illiteracy and young people

In 1917 only around 32 per cent of the population of the Russian Empire could read and write.

Lenin believed that ending illiteracy was crucial to building socialism.

The reduction of illiteracy

Over time, there were a variety of policies that helped encourage literacy.

Literacy and the Civil War

During the Civil War:
- Trotsky introduced literacy classes throughout the Red Army. In 1918, 50 per cent of soldiers were illiterate, but by 1925 all soldiers were literate.
- Lunacharsky set up a network of Reading Rooms, or *likpunkty* (liquidation points), across Russia. They offered six-week intensive courses in reading and writing.

Outside the Red Army the literacy campaign was not a success. Learning was not a priority for those trying to survive the Civil War.

Literacy and the NEP

The campaign to end illiteracy was re-started in 1925, once the economy had stabilised. The government committed itself to eradicating illiteracy among adults by 1927. Communists worked with trade unions to establish libraries and run literacy classes. There were some successes:
- The Metal Workers' Union reported a decline in illiteracy from 14 per cent in 1925 to 4 per cent in 1926.
- The Transport Workers' Union achieved 99 per cent literacy by 1927.

Overall, literacy rates improved from 38 per cent in 1914 to 55 per cent in 1928. However, spreading literacy in rural areas was much harder.

Literacy under Stalin

In 1930 the Communist Party set the target of eliminating illiteracy by the end of the first Five-Year Plan. Stalin's campaign against illiteracy was run in a military style. Volunteer 'cultural soldiers', organised in 'cultural battalions', were sent into Soviet villages and told to fight a 'cultural war' against illiteracy. However, the campaign took place in the midst of forced collectivisation (see page 26). As a result, teachers were associated with the government and therefore peasants resisted the new teachers. Indeed, 40 per cent of teachers were physically attacked in the first year of the campaign.

The campaign failed to eliminate illiteracy during the first Five-Year Plan. Nonetheless, by 1939 over 94 per cent of Soviet citizens were literate.

Communist young people's groups

In addition to schooling, the Communists set up groups for young people:
- The Young Pioneers was established in 1922 to cater for children between the ages of 10 and 15.
- Komsomol was founded in 1918 for people between the ages of 16 and 28.

Komsomol and the Young Pioneers in the 1920s

Komsomol members and the Young Pioneers wore a uniform and took part in activities such as camping and hiking. They also had talks from local factory workers, soldiers from the Red Army and farm workers.

In theory Komsomol members were meant to be disciplined and keen supporters of the Communist Party. However, in reality they often had a reputation for drunkenness, promiscuity and hooliganism.

Youth groups under Stalin

During the 1930s members of Komsomol and the Young Pioneers were expected to spy on their parents and report any criminal behaviour to the police. Youth groups encouraged young people to be hard-working and obedient.

Youth groups, 1954–85

Khrushchev had a lot of faith in youth organisations. He was keen to involve Komsomol members in his initiatives. For example, he hoped that Komsomol would play a leading role in holding factory managers and Party officials to account, reminding them of the vision that they were all working towards.

Brezhnev, by contrast, was suspicious of Komsomol. He viewed Komsomol's leadership as young and ambitious, and therefore potentially dangerous. He believed that Komsomol should keep young people disciplined and obedient and emphasise the values of working hard and respect for the government.

Spectrum of importance

Below are a sample exam question and a list of general points, which could be used to answer the question. Use your own knowledge and the information on the previous pages to reach a judgement about the importance of these general points to the question posed. Write numbers on the spectrum below to indicate their relative importance, in terms of how far the Communists controlled each area of life. Having done this, write a brief justification of your placement, explaining why some of these factors are more important than others. The resulting diagram could form the basis of an essay plan.

> To what extent was government control over the lives of the people maintained in the years 1918–53?

1   Control of young people through Young Pioneers and Komsomol
2   Control of working life through collectivisation and Five-Year Plans
3   Control of politics through the one-party state and terror
4   Control of the media through censorship and propaganda

←──→

Least important   Most important

You're the examiner

Below are a sample exam question and a paragraph written in answer to this question. Read the paragraph and the mark scheme provided on page 99. Decide which level you would award the paragraph. Write the level below, along with a justification for your choice.

> How successful were Communist education policies in the years 1918–53?

Communist education policies were extremely successful in terms of reducing illiteracy in the period 1918–53. The ultimate goal of Soviet literacy policy was to end illiteracy. Initially the policy failed, in the sense that it failed to eliminate illiteracy during the Civil War due to the need to prioritise military victory. The policy also failed in the sense that the government failed to meet its target of eliminating illiteracy by 1927. However, the government did make progress in the 1920s, for example, 99 per cent of transport workers were literate by 1927, and all Red Army soldiers were literate by 1925. Real progress was made under Stalin, and by 1939 over 94 per cent of Soviet citizens were literate, and illiteracy had been completely eradicated by 1953. Therefore, in terms of ending illiteracy Communist education policies were extremely successful because, in spite of a difficult start, by 1953 the government had achieved its goal of 100 per cent literacy.

Level:

Mark:

Reason for choosing this level and this mark:

_____

_____

Education: the curriculum

The Communists had high hopes for education. However, during the Civil War there were insufficient resources to achieve their goal of providing free polytechnic education to all children between 8 and 17.

Schooling, 1917–28

Before 1921 winning the Civil War was more important to the government than education. Therefore, many schools were requisitioned by the army and turned into stores or barracks, meaning that in some areas education ceased.

During the NEP, schooling expanded. From 1927 fees for primary schools were abolished, and from then on the majority of children received a four-year primary education. By 1928 about 60 per cent of Soviet children of primary school age were in school, around 10 per cent more than prior to the revolution.

Secondary education was largely unreformed, and received limited central funding. Therefore, only children from wealthy families got a full secondary education.

State control of the curriculum under Stalin

Education expanded under Stalin. At the same time, the government established tight control over the curriculum.

Curriculum reform

Stalin's educational goal was to create a new generation of disciplined and patriotic Soviet citizens who could work effectively in Soviet factories. Therefore, Stalin's curriculum, introduced in the early 1930s, focused on:
- core subjects such as reading, writing, maths and science
- the history of 'great men' and national heroes such as Ivan the Terrible and Peter the Great
- strictly regimented discipline.

Education under Stalin

Primary education expanded significantly under Stalin. By 1953 official figures showed:
- Almost 100 per cent of 8 to 12 year olds gained the full four years of primary education.
- Around 65 per cent of 12 to 17 year olds gained some secondary education.
- Around 20 per cent of 15 to 17 year olds completed secondary education.

University education also expanded from 170,000 students in 1927 to 1.5 million in 1953.

Educational inequalities under Stalin

Access to secondary school and university was still limited. Fees were maintained in the higher levels of education to keep educational costs down. Significantly, the Communist Party and trade unions offered scholarships and grants to help students access higher education. However, the system favoured the sons and daughters of Party officials.

Educational reform and expansion, 1953–85

Khrushchev believed that education, along with much else in the Soviet Union, was in need of reform. However, his reforms were unpopular and therefore Brezhnev restored much of the Stalinist curriculum after Khrushchev's fall.

Khrushchev's reforms

Khrushchev was determined to improve schooling. Therefore he:
- merged small country schools to improve standards in rural areas
- doubled the number of schools in towns and cities.
- invested in teacher training and recruitment; reducing class sizes improved education
- abolished fees for students attending secondary schools from 1956
- shifted the balance of the curriculum away from the traditional subjects towards vocational training
- replaced exams with continuous assessment
- ended the right of head teachers to expel students.

Education, 1964–85

Senior Communists believed that Khrushchev's reforms undermined the academic excellence of the Soviet system. Therefore, Brezhnev's top educational priority was to reverse Khrushchev's educational reforms. Under Brezhnev:
- A more traditional curriculum was reinstated.
- Vocational training of 16- to 19-year-old students in factories and farms was ended.

Textbooks were updated in the 1970s to reflect the latest scientific discoveries. However, the curriculum remained largely unchanged through the 1970s and early 1980s. Indeed, by 1985 students were still required to study the same mix of subjects established in 1947.

Identify the concept **a**

Below are five sample exam questions based on some of the following concepts:

- cause – questions concern the reasons for something, or why something happened
- consequence – questions concern the impact of an event, an action or a policy
- change/continuity – questions ask you to investigate the extent to which things changed or stayed the same
- similarity/difference – questions ask you to investigate the extent to which two events, actions or policies were similar
- significance – questions concern the importance of an event, an action or a policy.

Read each of the questions and work out which of the concepts they are based on.

1 How far do you agree that Soviet family life was transformed in the years 1918–64?

2 How successful were Soviet educational policies in the years 1953–85?

3 To what extent were there changes in Soviet social policy in the years 1918–64? **AS**

4 Were Khrushchev's economic reforms the main reason for the decline in the Soviet economy in the years 1953–85? Explain your answer. **AS**

5 How accurate is it to say that there was very little difference in the social and economic policies of Communist governments under Khrushchev and Brezhnev?

Developing an argument

Below are a sample exam question, a list of key points to be made in the essay, and a paragraph from the essay. Read the question, the plan and the sample paragraph. Rewrite the paragraph in order to develop an argument. Your paragraph should answer the question directly, and set out the evidence that supports your argument. Crucially, it should develop an argument by setting out a general answer to the question and reasons that support this.

How accurate is it to say that, in the years 1953–82, the government of the USSR was increasingly stable?

Key points:

- Improvements in social benefits under Khrushchev increased stability.
- Brezhnev's counter-reforms and his 'social contract' improved stability.
- Khrushchev's reforms partly destabilised Soviet government.
- Nonconformity, concerns about the government, and clashes with dissidents continued to 1982.

The government of the USSR was largely stable in the years 1953–82. However, the extent to which stability increased is debatable. Certainly, there were improvements in social benefits under Khrushchev, and Brezhnev's counter-reforms and his 'social contract' improved stability. However, some of Khrushchev's reforms partly destabilised Soviet government, and there were conflicts with nonconformists, clashes with dissidents and concerns about the stagnation and corruption of government up until 1982.

Exam focus

Below is a sample high-level essay. Read it and the comments around it.

To what extent was there a genuine improvement in the living standards of the Soviet people in the years 1953–85?

There was an undoubted improvement in the living standards of the Soviet people in the years 1953–85. In 1953, while the Soviet Union was an industrial giant with a powerful economy, welfare was still very basic, there was a housing crisis and food and consumer goods were scarce. Khrushchev and Brezhnev largely solved these problems. Nonetheless, in all of these areas there remained problems, and while living standards did improve they did so less than the government promised, and they improved for some more than others.

> The essay begins well with a clear focus on the question.

> The essay recognises a range of areas where living standards improved, as well as the problems experienced in the period.

There were clear improvements in welfare in the years 1953–85. By 1953 there was an essential welfare network. Healthcare was available to factory workers, and by 1947 vaccines were available for typhus and malaria for all Soviet citizens. At the same time, free food was available from factory canteens. However, things improved dramatically under Khrushchev. Compared to 1950 Khrushchev doubled the healthcare budget making healthcare available to farmers as well as workers. Additionally, he extended free food to school canteens in the country and the city. Khrushchev went further, introducing free public transport and pensions. Under Brezhnev, welfare was extended so that Soviet citizens received subsidised electricity and water; indeed, most utilities were provided almost free of charge. Holidays were subsidised and spending on healthcare increased every year. Clearly, living standards improved for all Soviet citizens in the years 1953–85 because Khrushchev extended welfare benefits to farmers, and Khrushchev and Brezhnev extended welfare provision across more and more areas of Soviet life.

> This paragraph begins with an effective contrast between welfare in 1953 and the improvements that followed.

> The paragraph ends with an effective piece of analysis, evaluating how far welfare improved.

Khrushchev and Brezhnev solved the housing crisis that had grown worse under Stalin. In 1953 many families were forced to live in *kommunalka*, sharing only 4 or 5 square metres of space. Khrushchev transformed the situation, building prefabricated concrete blocks, which allowed families to have an entire flat with running water and central heating. This method of building and the K-7 block, or *Khrushchyovka*, allowed apartment blocks to be constructed quickly and easily. The K-7 was designed to be a temporary solution to the housing crisis, before more luxurious houses were built. The government began constructing K-7 blocks in the 1950s. However, K-7s were constructed throughout the 1980s. The construction of the K-7s was an effective solution to the housing crisis, and it improved the standard of living of the vast majority of Soviet citizens as it allowed families to live in modern, spacious accommodation. However, after the 1960s living and housing standards did not continue improving, as Khrushchev's promise of even more luxurious housing was never realised.

> Focus is maintained throughout the essay by clear points.

> The paragraph contains well-selected detail that helps support the point of the paragraph.

Living standards improved dramatically because of a significant improvement in the availability of food. Stalin's policy of collectivisation had been a failure in the sense that it made farms inefficient and provided little incentive to increase the production of food, making food scarce and expensive. Khrushchev sought to solve the problem with food by investing in agriculture. He increased production incentives, which raised farm incomes by 250 per cent between 1952 and 1956. He also initiated the Virgin Lands Scheme, which created new farms in the northern Caucasus, Kazakhstan, and western Siberia. As a result, there was a 35.3 per cent increase in food production from 1954 to 58. This improved the food situation, but there were still shortages. Brezhnev was able to increase food consumption by importing grain from the West to keep food prices low. Through a mixture of investment under Khrushchev and imports under Brezhnev the living standards of Soviet citizens clearly improved because food prices dropped and food became more plentiful after 1953.

> The paragraph contains precise detail.

Finally, living standards improved because of improvements in the availability of consumer goods. Under Stalin the economy focused on heavy industry and defence. Consequently, by 1953 while the economy was growing fast the supply of consumer goods was limited. Khrushchev boosted the production of consumer goods by investing in light industry. As a result, living standards improved as production of radios, refrigerators, washing machines and televisions increased. However, living standards were still lower than in Western European countries. For example, by 1966 only five out of a thousand people owned cars in the Soviet Union, compared to 200 in a thousand in the UK. The availability of consumer goods improved further under Brezhnev, because he allowed the development of the 'second economy', which allowed Soviet citizens to buy consumer goods illegally. However, only privileged citizens could afford Western goods, and there were continual shortages of popular consumer goods. Indeed, the incomes of farmers still lagged behind the incomes of urban workers, and the incomes of women were still lower than those of men, meaning that large sections of Soviet society were unable to buy popular goods. In this way, while there were significant improvements in the standard of living due to the availability of consumer goods, there were still problems in terms of shortages, even in 1985.

> The paragraph extends the range of the essay by considering a fourth factor.

In conclusion, there was genuine improvement in the living standards in the years 1953–85 because the Stalin years of basic welfare, housing crisis and shortages was replaced by a more advanced welfare system, decent housing for all citizens and relative affluence. However, there were shortcomings, which meant that living standards did not rise equally for all. Farmers on low wages had no access to the luxuries that were available to privileged city dwellers through the 'second market'. Nonetheless, there was a genuine improvement in the essential aspects of life, as all citizens were guaranteed good healthcare, decent housing and cheap food. In this sense, there was a genuine improvement in the essentials for all, but privileged citizens in the cities benefited most of all.

> The conclusion considers the meaning of 'genuine improvement', setting out criteria for judgement.

> The conclusion reaches a judgement about the extent of improvement by contrasting the extent of improvement for all with the extent of improvement for privileged citizens.

This essay achieves a mark in Level 4 as it analyses a range of key issues relevant to the extent of improvement in living standards. It also deploys sufficient knowledge to fully answer the question. It uses valid criteria to substantiate an overall judgement. However, the analysis is not sustained and the criteria are introduced very late in the essay, meaning that it does not get a mark in the very highest level.

Moving from a Level 4 to Level 5

The exam focus essay at the end of Section 1 (pages 18–19) provided a Level 5 essay. The essay here achieves a Level 4. Read both essays, and the comments provided. Make a list of the additional features required to push a Level 4 essay into Level 5.

AS Level questions

To what extent was Soviet social policy successful in the years 1918–53?

To what extent did the lives of Soviet citizens improve in the years 1928–64?

Was the illumination of illiteracy the main consequence of the Communist social policy in the years 1918–53? Explain your answer.

5 What explains the fall of the USSR, c.1985–91?

The economic weaknesses of the USSR

Historians have disagreed about the reasons for the fall of the USSR. Some of the main reasons given by historians include:

- the significance of the economic weaknesses of the USSR and the failure of reform
- the effects of **Gorbachev**'s failure to reform the Communist Party and the Soviet government
- the impact of the nationalist resurgence in the late 1980s in the Soviet Republics and in the communist states of Eastern Europe
- the roles of Gorbachev and **Yeltsin**.

The USSR and the Communist Party

The USSR comprised 15 Republics. In this sense, the USSR was a **supranational** organisation, rather than a nation. The Communist Party governed the whole of the Union, holding it together.

Long-term economic problems

Some historians argue that long-term economic weaknesses played a part in the collapse of the USSR.

Centralisation

The centralised nature of the Soviet economy meant that it was profoundly inefficient. Government administrators based in Moscow were unable to co-ordinate the economy effectively:

- Fertilisers and pesticides often arrived at the wrong time, hampering crop growth.
- Factories received the wrong grade of products like steel and oil.
- It was difficult to get hold of spare parts, as administrators were unable to meet the detailed needs of factory managers.

Central control created problems across the whole country.

Problems in industry

Soviet industry was flawed in the following ways:

- The Soviet economy failed to create incentives for hard work or innovation. Therefore, Soviet workers were less productive than Western workers.
- Gosplan set targets for production quantity, but not quality. Therefore, the Soviet economy tended to produce poor quality or useless goods.

Problems in agriculture

Soviet agriculture required a much greater proportion of the population than US agriculture and yet American farms were six times more productive.

Soviet infrastructure

Soviet infrastructure was consistently inadequate.

- The Soviet transport system had never been fully modernised. Therefore, transporting food around the country was difficult.
- A lack of modern storage facilities meant that a lot of what was produced was wasted. For example, grain often rotted.

Military expenditure

Economic growth and modernisation was also hampered by Soviet military spending. Between 1965 and 1985 the proportion of Gross Domestic Product (GDP) spent on defence increased from around 12 per cent to 17 per cent. This was a much greater burden than US defence spending, which averaged around 6 per cent over the same period. Moreover, defence spending starved other areas of the economy, meaning that the USSR could not invest in modern infrastructure or farming.

How significant were long-term problems?

By 1985 the Soviet economy had essentially stopped growing. However, some historians argue that there was no real crisis. The Soviet economy had functioned inefficiently for decades, and could have continued to do so. From this point of view, while long-term problems undermined the USSR, they were not the primary cause of collapse.

Contrasting interpretations

Below are a sample Section C exam question and the accompanying extracts. The extracts offer different interpretations of the issue raised by the question. Identify the interpretation offered in each extract and complete the table below, indicating how far the extracts agree with each other, and explaining your answer.

	Extent of agreement	Justification
Extracts 1 and 2		

In the light of differing interpretations, how convincing do you find the view that the economy played a central role in the fall of the USSR (Extract 1)?

Study Extracts 1 and 2. Historians have different views about the reasons for the fall of the Soviet Union. Analyse and evaluate the extracts and use your knowledge of the issues to explain your answer to the following question. How far do you agree with the view that the collapse of the Soviet Union came about because of the economic weaknesses of the USSR? **AS**

EXTRACT 1

Maximilian Spinner, *The Breakdown of the USSR*, published in 2007

The collapse of the Soviet Union has been one of the most controversial issues discussed among historians. In order to understand the collapse of Communism in the Soviet Union, a central role must be given to the economy and its effect on other areas. Most symptoms of the crisis and the ultimate breakdown of the system can in fact be attributed to the impact of economic failure. Whereas economic modernisation was the motor of success in the earlier decades of the Soviet Union, the economy became the weakest link of the Soviet system.

Under Brezhnev 'consolidating socialism' was declared the official aim, while catching up with the west or even overtaking it became unrealistic. In reality 'consolidating socialism' reflected stagnation in the economy. Economic stagnation created an ideological dilemma. The Party was increasingly guiding the country into economic decline rather than into a bright future. Economic success was the most important source of legitimacy for the Soviet Union.

EXTRACT 2

Martin McCauley, *The Rise and Fall of the Soviet Union*, published in 2014

The collapse was the result of unintended consequences of government policies. The economy played a key role here. In an attempt to stimulate a slowing economy, the leadership adopted policies which fatally weakened the political and ideological pillars which sustained the system. This brought down the whole edifice. Hence the economic crisis did not cause the collapse of the Soviet Union. The economic situation after 1992 was worse but this did not lead to the demise of post-communist Russia. Ill-advised political decision making was the key variable.

The conclusion is that poor leadership provoked political and economic collapse. A major weakness was the Party-state system. The Party never possessed the technical expertise to run the country. That should have been the role of the government. Instead the Party was always setting goals and interfering in the economy. Gorbachev's attempts at economic reform provoked a collapse. One of the reasons for this was that economic reform needs time to produce positive results. Gorbachev was impatient and introduced more radical reforms to accelerate growth. He eventually wrecked the system.

The failure of economic reform, 1985–90

Some historians argue that the failure of Gorbachev's economic policy was the main reason for the fall of the USSR. Nonetheless, historians disagree over the nature of the failure:

- Some historians argue that Gorbachev's policies failed because they undermined the existing system.
- Others argue that Gorbachev's economic policies failed because he kept changing his approach, therefore his policies never had time to develop.
- Some historians argue that inherent weaknesses meant that the Soviet economy could not be saved. Therefore, the failure of Gorbachev's reforms was inevitable.

Gorbachev's policy

Gorbachev's policy was designed to address the problems with the Soviet economy. Under Gorbachev Soviet economic policy went through three stages.

- Rationalisation: the period from 1985 to 86, where Gorbachev tried to improve the way in which the command economy worked.
- Reform: the period from late 1986 to 1990 in which Gorbachev attempted to introduce some market measures into the existing command economy in order to create an economy that had the best features of socialism and capitalism.
- Transformation: the period from 1990 to 91, in which Gorbachev abandoned the command economy and tried to introduce a market economy.

Rationalisation, 1985–86

Gorbachev's first set of economic measures did not alter the fundamental nature of the economy. Between 1985 and 1986 Gorbachev:

- continued Andropov's anti-alcohol campaign, cutting state production of alcohol by 50 per cent
- introduced *uskorenie* or 'acceleration', a programme of investment designed to modernise the economy.

Early failures

Gorbachev's first measures failed. The anti-alcohol campaign failed as Soviet citizens simply bought alcohol illegally. Consequently, the government made much less money out of vodka sales, and Soviet citizens continued to drink. Alcohol revenues dropped by 67 billion roubles (9 per cent of GDP). As a result, the campaign was abandoned in 1988.

Acceleration failed for two reasons.

- Firstly, it was funded by borrowing money from Western governments. Government debt rose from $18.1 billion in 1981 to $27.2 billion in 1988, leading to growing inflation.
- Secondly, Gorbachev invested in energy production, ignoring the advice of experts who argued for more investment in high-tech machines. Therefore, the investment did not lead to greater growth.

Reform, 1987–90

The failure of acceleration led Gorbachev to begin experiments with market reforms. He passed a series of laws to allow market forces to play a bigger role in the economy.

- The Law on Individual Economic Activity (November 1986) made it legal for individuals to make money by doing small-scale jobs such as private teaching or repairs and maintenance.
- The Law on State Enterprises (June 1987) devolved power from central government to factory management, allowing factory managers to set the prices for the goods they produced.
- The Law on co-operatives (May 1988) made it legal to set up large co-operatives, which functioned like private companies.

Failure of market reform

Gorbachev's market reforms created growing economic chaos. The reforms undermined the central planning system, while at the same time failing to create an effective market alternative. As a result, there was no effective way of distributing goods, and shortages of essential goods became increasingly severe. For example, although Soviet farms had produced 218 million tons of grain in 1990 there was no longer an effective distribution system and therefore there were major shortages.

Political consequences

By 1990 economic problems led to political problems. Government figures showed that between 1986 and 1990 GDP had shrunk by 4 per cent. What is more, prices were rising. Additionally, senior Party members were growing rich, as they were able to seize control of economic assets, which were being privatised. Consequently, approval ratings dropped, strikes increased and there was a sharp decline in support for the Communist Party.

RAG – rate the extract

Below are a sample Section C exam question and one of the extracts referred to in the question. Read the question, study the extract and, using three coloured pens, underline it in red, amber or green to show:

- Red: the interpretation offered by the source
- Amber: evidence that supports this interpretation
- Green: counter-arguments and counter-evidence provided by the source

In the light of differing interpretations, how convincing do you find the view that the USSR fell because of the failure of Gorbachev's economic reforms?

EXTRACT 1:

From Martin McCauley, *Economic Weaknesses and the Failure of Reform*, published in 2014

Gorbachev did not understand how the Soviet planned economy functioned. His advisers were over confident and their recipes for growth often had the opposite effect. Moving from a command to a market economy was something which had previously never been considered. Gorbachev was perplexed by the failure of the reforms. There was a belief that a reform borrowed from a market economy – for example, enterprise self-financing – could be grafted on to a command economy and the result would be the best of both worlds, socialist and capitalist. A magic mix of the best of capitalist and socialist policies would work miracles. However, monetary (the emission of money and credit) and fiscal (taxation) policy was loose and inevitably led to high inflation. Hence financial reforms from the centre in 1990 and 1991 had little effect.

China and Vietnam have demonstrated that it is possible to move from a command to a market economy without undermining the power of the Communist Party. Hence the reasons for the failure of economic reform are political. Gorbachev removed the ideological and political pillars on which the Soviet Union was built. As a result, the whole edifice collapsed.

Add own knowledge

Using the extract from the last activity write relevant own knowledge that would help you answer the question around the extract's edge.

Tips:

- You can add your own knowledge that supports *and challenges* the extract.
- You can also add new alternative arguments that challenge the interpretation offered by the extract.

The failure of economic reform, 1990–91

By 1990 Gorbachev abandoned attempts to save the Soviet command economy. Rather, he began to introduce a market economy. Gorbachev became caught in the midst of a political battle between hardliners who wanted to preserve the Soviet economic and political system and radicals who wanted to speed up reform.

Transformation, 1990–91

In order to minimise the economic problems that were expected during the transition to a market economy, Gorbachev and Boris Yeltsin commissioned two Soviet economists, Stanislav Shatalin and Grigory Yavlinsky, to devise a plan for the economic transformation. The result was the '500 Day Programme', published in August 1990. Shatalin and Yavlinsky proposed widespread privatisation and complete marketisation in less than two years.

Political problems

Gorbachev initially supported the proposals, but under pressure from senior hardline Communists he backed down. Nonetheless, he remained committed to an economic transformation, but was persuaded that it should happen at a slower pace.

Final reforms

In January 1991 the **Supreme Soviet** introduced private property, as an important step towards a free market economy. As a result, the Soviet people could own land and factories in a way that had been impossible since the 1920s. In April, a law was passed to allow citizens to trade stocks and shares. Again, this reform was designed to revitalise the economy through the introduction of market forces.

However, the economy continued to decline. Oil production fell by 9 per cent, while steel and tractor production both fell by 12 per cent. An official government report stated that the Soviet economy was moving beyond crisis to catastrophe.

By the summer of 1991 the Soviet government and Republican governments were effectively bankrupt. Neither had the economic power to govern. Consequently, although Yeltsin announced a programme of full marketisation in October 1991, it was difficult to implement.

Interpretation: economics and the fall of the USSR

Historians disagree over the significance of economic problems in the fall of the USSR.
- Some argue that Gorbachev's reforms created economic chaos, which in turn led to a political crisis, and caused the collapse of the USSR.
- Others claim that the Soviet economy was bound to disintegrate because of its long-term weaknesses. From this point of view Gorbachev's reforms merely sped up the inevitable economic collapse.
- Finally, some historians argue that Gorbachev's economic reforms could have been successful. According to this interpretation, Gorbachev's mistake was to introduce economic reforms and political reforms at the same time, as political freedoms allowed Soviet citizens to organise in protest against the government when the economy began to fail. Indeed, historians who make this argument point to the success of economic reform in China, where economic reform took place without political liberalisation.

Challenge the historian

Below are a sample Section C exam question and one of the accompanying extracts. You must read the extract, identify the interpretation it offers, and use your own knowledge to provide a counter-argument, challenging the extract's interpretation.

> In the light of differing interpretations, how convincing do you find the view that 'Gorbachev's over-confident leadership' led to the fall of the Soviet Union?

Interpretation offered by the source:

_____

Counter-argument:

_____

_____

EXTRACT 1

From Michael J. Oliver and Derek Howard Aldcroft, *Economic Disasters of the Twentieth Century*, published in 2008.

While the Soviet economic model suffered from inherent flaws, these were not the fundamental cause of collapse. As the command economy floundered, tantalizing glimpses of Western capitalism seeped through via increasing trade and the black market, providing hope of a better future for ordinary Soviet citizens.

By the early 1980s woefully bad economic signs forced the Soviet leadership to embrace radical policies. Under Gorbachev's over-confident leadership, the introduction of a heady mixture of political and economic reforms fatally undermined the Soviet system and ensured its ultimate collapse.

The de-escalation of the Cold War, and the fact that the Soviet government was no longer willing or able to make the economic sacrifices necessary to help sustain its dominance over Eastern Europe brought the Eastern Bloc crashing down. Two years later the Soviet Union followed.

Recommended reading

Below is a list of suggested further reading on this topic.

- *The Cambridge History of Russia*, Volume X, pages 316–351, Ronald Grigor Suny (2008)
- *Russian Politics and Society*, Fourth Edition, pages 25–39, Richard Sakwa (2008)
- *Comrades!*, pages 448–458, Robert Service (2007)

Gorbachev's reform of the Party and government

Some historians argue that the main reason for the fall of the USSR was the failure of Gorbachev's political reforms.

Gorbachev's goals

Gorbachev had a series of reasons for wanting to reform the Party and the government.

- First, as a Communist, he was committed to the creation of a democracy for working people. Gorbachev knew that Lenin's single-party state was designed to be temporary, and that Lenin's long-term goal was to create a highly democratic society.
- Secondly, Gorbachev knew that some Party members were corrupt and inefficient. He hoped that a measure of democracy would allow the Soviet people to play a role in purging the Party.
- Thirdly, Gorbachev wanted greater freedom of speech so that experts could contribute to building socialism in the USSR.
- Finally, Gorbachev was aware that under Brezhnev a large proportion of the Soviet population had become cynical about Communist rule, believing that the Communist Party had become corrupt. Gorbachev hoped that allowing people to participate in government would end the cynicism of the Soviet people by showing that the Communists were serious about reform.

Generally, Gorbachev hoped that a degree of political reform would revitalise the USSR.

The dangers of reform

However, Gorbachev was also aware of the dangers of reform. Gorbachev knew that Khrushchev's reforms had led to demands for multi-party democracy and an end to Communist rule.

Undermining the Communist Party threatened to destroy the USSR, as the Communist Party was the organisation that held the Union together.

Gorbachev's early reforms

In 1985 Gorbachev's plans for reform were quite limited. In essence he wanted to:
- open up debate within the Party
- allow intellectuals more freedom of expression
- allow the public to have more access to information.

Purging the party

One of Gorbachev's first reforms was to purge the Party of senior Communists who had served under Brezhnev. This allowed Gorbachev to appoint a new generation of ministers who favoured reform. For example, he made Nikolai Ryzhkov Prime Minister and appointed Viktor Chebrikov head of the KGB and Boris Yeltsin head of the Communist Party in Moscow.

Glasnost, 1986–88

In 1986 Gorbachev launched **glasnost**, a policy of openness. Gorbachev repeatedly stated that the government needed to admit the truth. As a result of glasnost, information about economics and Soviet history became more readily available. Moreover, there was a liberalisation of the media.

- In 1986, Gorbachev gave Aleksandr Yakovlev responsibility for the Soviet media. Yakovlev appointed new radical editors.
- In 1988, the Soviet press published criticisms of Marx and Lenin.
- From 1988 citizens were permitted to listen to foreign radio broadcasts and read foreign newspapers
- From 1988 the Communist Party revealed the scale of the economic problems facing the USSR.

The political effects of Gorbachev's reforms

Gorbachev's political reforms profoundly weakened the Party.
- They divided the Party. Many Communist officials refused to support Gorbachev's political and economic reforms. Hardliners believed that glasnost and *Perestroika* would end the power of the Party and the privileges of Party members. In short, they feared reform would risk destroying the Communist system.
- Factions emerged – hardliners and moderates resisted reform while radicals embraced it.
- Revelations about the economy and about the extent of Stalin's terror meant that many citizens lost faith in the government.
- A freer media also allowed opponents of Communism to undermine the government by publishing criticisms.

Rather than reviving the system, Gorbachev's reforms undermined Communism by dividing the Party and exposing the government to criticism.

Write the question **a**

The following extracts relate to the causes of the collapse of the Soviet Union. Having read the previous pages about the Soviet Union's collapse write a Section C exam-style question to accompany the extracts.

Study Extracts 1 and 2. In the light of differing interpretations, how convincing do you find the view that

_____

_____

To explain your answer, analyse and evaluate the material in both extracts, using your own knowledge of the issues.

Study Extracts 1 and 2. Historians have different views about the reasons for the fall of the Soviet Union. Analyse and evaluate the extracts and use your knowledge of the issues to explain your answer to the following question. How far do you agree with the view that **AS**

_____

_____

EXTRACT 1

From Richard Sakwa, *Gorbachev's Political Reforms*, published in 2015

Why did a system collapse so quickly and suddenly? The fundamental reason is Mikhail Gorbachev's botched attempt to reform the political system. The Soviet Union could have continued if Gorbachev had not removed the keystone in the arch, the Communist Party of the Soviet Union (CPSU) and its 'apparatus' (apparat), the gigantic machinery of government.

Gorbachev came to power in March 1985 not to destroy the Soviet system of governance but to save it. However, as *perestroika* gathered pace his reforms became increasingly radical, and instead of simply reforming communism, Gorbachev sought to create a new system that is conventionally called 'reform communism', which he defined as 'humane, democratic socialism'. This ended up provoking numerous contradictions. The overall principal aim was to create a 'socialist legal state', with the separation of powers and a genuine parliament. However, the system ended up trapped between a disrupted old Soviet system of governance and a new system that could not be established. The steering mechanism of the state was destroyed but no effective alternative system was put in place, and by the end of 1991 the whole order collapsed.

EXTRACT 2

From Stephen Richards Graubard, *Exit from Communism*, published in 1998

Gorbachev's major failure was economic reform. Keenly aware of the need for economic reform he never realised that no middle way existed. As a result, his economic policies tended to fall between two stools, leading to a completely inconsistent economic system, utterly out of balance.

The Soviet economic system became far worse than it would have been under an ordinary command economy, or a bold step forward to complete market economy. Initially, Gorbachev was impeded by Communist conservatives, but from 1990 on he showed that he was unprepared to go very far himself. At the very end he insisted on slow change. He failed to grasp that disintegration and chaos had already been reached and that speedy action was the requirement of the day.

The failure of Gorbachev's political reforms

From 1988 Gorbachev began a process that he called democratisation. Some historians argue that this profoundly weakened Communist rule and in so doing led to the collapse of the USSR.

Reforms, 1988

The Nineteenth Party Conference of 1988 introduced radical reforms to the government. The Party Conference authorised multi-candidate elections to the Soviets. This meant that Soviet citizens could choose between rival Communist candidates and elect either radicals or moderates.

Election, 1989

The first multi-candidate election took place in March 1989. For the first time since 1921 Communists had to campaign for election.

Several high-ranking Communists were defeated, including five members of the Central Committee. Radicals, on the other hand, did well. Yeltsin won with 89 per cent of the vote in Moscow.

Republic elections, 1990

The Republic elections of March 1990 also weakened the Communist Party:

- In Moscow, for example, a group called Democratic Russia won 85 per cent of the seats.
- In Leningrad the group Democratic Elections 90, another new anti-Communist group, took 80 per cent of the seats.

Gorbachev had assumed that democratisation would strengthen the radicals within the Communist Party. However, they weakened the whole of the Party.

The consequences of the reforms

Overall, the 1989 and 1990 elections weakened the Communist Party.

- The 1989 election also led to the formation of the Inter-Regional Deputies' Group (IRDG), led by Boris Yeltsin and Andrei Sakharov. The IRDG was, effectively, an opposition group to the Communists. Therefore, this was the first time since 1921 that an opposition group was organised.

- Nationalists who wanted to break up the USSR used the election to campaign for independence. In Georgia, these campaigns resulted in violence (see page 76).
- Yeltsin emerged from the election as a popular figure and a rival to Gorbachev. Indeed, Yeltsin's desire to replace the USSR with a loose confederation of truly independent states was extremely popular with nationalists across the USSR, and therefore a threat to the Union.

Gorbachev had assumed that democratisation would strengthen the radicals within the Communist Party. However, the Soviet elections weakened the whole of the Party, increasing the authority of anti-Party and nationalist groups.

Constitutional reform

Democratisation had succeeded in weakening the Communist Party. However, it had not produced a strong government. Therefore, in 1990 Gorbachev introduced constitutional reforms to give himself new powers to deal with the USSR's growing economic and political problems.

The presidency

Gorbachev's new constitution created the position of President of the USSR. The new president would be appointed by the Congress of People's Deputies. Gorbachev hoped that being appointed president would give him new authority.

Following his appointment Gorbachev was given emergency powers for 18 months in order to deal with the economic crisis, and with growing unrest in the Republics.

Gorbachev's legitimacy

Gorbachev's appointment as president did not solve his problems. In essence, Gorbachev's new position was unelected, and therefore he did not have the legitimacy that elected politicians could claim.

Identify the interpretation

Below are a sample Section C exam question and the two accompanying extracts. The extracts offer different interpretations of the issue raised by the question. Read the extracts and underline the key interpretations in each extract.

In the light of differing interpretations, how convincing do you find the view that the USSR fell because Gorbachev's reforms 'fatally undermined the Communist Party' (Extract 1)?

Study Extracts 1 and 2. Historians have different views about the reasons for the fall of the Soviet Union. Analyse and evaluate the extracts and use your knowledge of the issues to explain your answer to the following question. How far do you agree with the view that the collapse of the Soviet Union came about because Gorbachev's political reforms undermined the Communist Party? **AS**

EXTRACT 1

From Robert Strayer, *Why Did the Soviet Union Collapse?* published in 1997

Between 1987 and 1990, Gorbachev engineered something close to a political miracle. Competitive elections, a real working parliament, the end of the party's political monopoly, and the creation of a powerful presidency – all had occurred within a few years, with the party's reluctant consent, and without a violent backlash. How did this happen? Particularly at the beginning everyone recognised the need for some change, and Gorbachev consistently articulated his reforms within a socialist framework. Gorbachev's genuine popularity in the country, at least up to mid-1989, and the considerable growth of a democratic movement urging even more radical policies provided pressure for democratization.

But at the same time those victories for political reform bypassed, diminished, divided, and demoralised the Communist Party. Here, clearly, is one of the central elements in the collapse of the Soviet Union. Gorbachev felt compelled to attack and weaken the party in order to implement his reform program, but in doing so he fatally undermined the Communist Party, the single institution that had bound the country together.

EXTRACT 2

From Archie Brown, *The Gorbachev Era*, published in 2006

There is no doubt that the attempt to reform the Soviet economy ended in failure. Part of the reason for that was the tension between reforming an existing system to make it work better and replacing that system by one which had a quite different logic. In the early years of *perestroika* the first aim was being pursued – and with only very limited success. By 1990–1, while there was not a consensus, there was at least a broad body of support among specialists for the idea that the command economy had to give way to a market economy. It was clearer to Gorbachev than to Yeltsin that this would mean tens of millions of citizens becoming worse off for some years to come. Freeing prices would improve the supply of goods and services but would also raise those prices to a level the majority could ill afford.

Much of the economic legislation of the *perestroika* years – not least the Law on Co-operatives – had helped to pave the way for marketisation, but the Soviet economy remained in limbo at the end of the Gorbachev era. It was no longer a functioning command economy but not yet a market system.

The nationalist resurgence of the late 1980s

The USSR was a supranational organisation that comprised 15 Republics. Within those Republics there were numerous national and ethnic groups. During the late 1980s and early 1990s there was a resurgence of nationalism that, some historians claim, led to the break-up of the USSR.

Gorbachev's reforms

Gorbachev's reforms had a significant impact on the Republics. Indeed, they led to a resurgence of nationalism.

Purges

One of Gorbachev's first actions was to purge the party of Brezhnev's supporters and Communist leaders he believed were corrupt. Brezhnev had encouraged the Communist Party to recruit local people in each Republic. Gorbachev's purge of local leaders was followed by the appointment of his own supporters. Gorbachev's supporters tended to be Russian. Russians also dominated at the top of government. Indeed, Gorbachev's Politburo, for example, only had one non-Russian member. In that sense, Gorbachev introduced a largely Russian leadership across the whole USSR, which sparked resentment in the Republics outside Russia.

Economic decline

Gorbachev's economic policies also caused problems in the Republics. Acceleration (see page 68) led to economic decline, which affected people across the USSR. Significantly, standards of living declined at the same time as Russian leaders took over. Therefore, people across the Republics blamed the new Russian leadership for their economic problems, whose reforms led to growing nationalism.

The impact of glasnost

Glasnost also led to the rise in nationalism.
- It exposed the ways in which Stalin's government had persecuted the USSR's ethnic minorities.
- It allowed Soviet people to see how much higher Western standards of living were than those within the USSR. Therefore, glasnost undermined the perception that the USSR had benefited people in the Republics.
- It allowed nationalist groups to publish material that demanded greater autonomy.

Growing unrest

Dissatisfaction with the USSR led to protest, unrest and violence.
- In 1988 nationalist protests broke out in Karabakh, a region of Azerbaijan. Competing demands of Armenian nationalists and Azerbaijani nationalists led to riots.
- In 1989 Uzbeks massacred the Muslim minority of Meskhetians. Soviet authorities were unable to restore peace in these areas, nor were they able to negotiate compromise. This led to a loss of faith in the Soviet government, which appeared incapable of either ensuring peace or meeting the demands of nationalists.
- In 1989 Georgian nationalists protested against the rights of the Abkhazian minority. On this occasion Soviet troops attempted to restore order by force. Consequently, Soviet forces killed 19 Georgian protestors and wounded thousands more. The killings, which became known as 'the Tbilisi Massacre', outraged Georgian nationalists.
- Nationalism also grew in Russia. The explosion at the Chernobyl nuclear power plant and the revelations of the devastating environmental impact of Communism on Russia led to the emergence of environmental groups. In Russia these groups sought to express their concerns in terms of saving the Russian landscape and saving the Russian environment.
- By 1988 large 'popular fronts' had emerged in the Baltic states. These movements were dedicated to gaining independence.

The consequences of growing nationalism

Nationalism weakened the USSR. It demonstrated that in many areas the Communist Party and the USSR had little popular support. Furthermore, it put the Party leadership in a difficult situation. Soviet forces were blamed for doing too little in some areas where they failed to prevent violence, or too much in other areas where they intervened with force. Either way, the popularity of the Party dwindled.

Summarise the interpretation

Below are a sample Section C exam question and the two accompanying extracts. The extracts offer different interpretations of the issue raised by the question. Below each extract, summarise the interpretation it offers.

In the light of differing interpretations, how convincing do you find the view that the fall of the USSR was because of 'the unintended result of Mikhail Gorbachev's policies' (Extract 1)?

Extract 1 argues

_____

_____

Extract 2 argues

_____

_____

Historians have different views about the reasons for the fall of the Soviet Union. Analyse and evaluate the extracts and use your knowledge of the issues to explain your answer to the following question. How far do you agree with the view that the collapse of the Soviet Union came about because of the consequences of Gorbachev's reforms? **AS**

EXTRACT 1

From Mark R. Beissinger, *Nationalism and the Collapse of Soviet Communism*, published in 2009

A number of works on the end of communism in the Soviet Union have argued that nationalism played only a minor role in the process, or that nationalism was a marginal motivation or influence on the actions of those involved in key decision-making. Failed politics and ideologies, an economy in decline, the burden of military competition with the United States and the corrupt *nomenklatura* instead loom large in these accounts. In many narratives of the end of communism, nationalism is portrayed merely as a consequence of communism's demise, not as a cause of the process of collapse itself.

Such a story, however, leaves a number of critical issues unaddressed. Within the Soviet Union enormous mobilisations involving millions of people occurred during these years, with nationalist demands being the most prominent among the banners under which people mobilised. It was the unintended result of Mikhail Gorbachev's policies – one that was made possible not just by the widening political freedom that glasnost afforded, but also by the nationalist forces that moved into that space and utilised it to overthrow the Soviet state.

EXTRACT 2

From Stephen F. Cohen, *Was the Soviet System Reformable?*, published in 2004

In reality, no anti-Soviet revolution from below ever took place, certainly not in Russia. In 1989–91, popular support for democratization and marketization was increasing, as were protests against Communist Party rule, corrupt elites, bureaucratic abuses, and economic shortages. But evidence of public support for the multinational Soviet state itself is clear. In an unprecedented referendum held in Russia and eight other republics in March 1991, which included 93 percent of the entire Soviet population, 76.4 percent of the very large turnout voted to preserve the Union–only nine months before it was abolished.

Nor is it true that a mass anti-Soviet "August Revolution" thwarted the attempted coup by hardline officials seeking to restore order throughout the country a few months after the referendum. Contrary to this equally widespread and specious myth, there was no "national resistance" to the putsch. Barely 1 percent of Soviet citizens actively opposed the three-day tank occupation even in pro-Yeltsin Moscow and considerably fewer resisted in provincial cities, the countryside, and outside the Russian Republic.

Nationalism in the USSR and the Eastern Bloc

The growth of nationalism within the USSR was linked to the emergence of independent nations in the Eastern Bloc. For some historians it was this combination of factors that best explains the fall of the USSR.

Nationalism in the Eastern Bloc

Gorbachev's change in policy towards the Communist 'satellite states' of the Eastern Bloc led to a growth in nationalism in the USSR. Under Stalin, Khrushchev and Brezhnev, countries in the Eastern Bloc were effectively controlled by the USSR. Gorbachev changed this with the Sinatra Doctrine.

The Sinatra Doctrine

In August 1989 Gorbachev renounced the USSR's 'right' to intervene in the affairs of other socialist countries. Rather, he argued that different countries could all follow their own path to Communism. This new doctrine, nicknamed the 'Sinatra Doctrine', after Frank Sinatra's song 'My Way', allowed much greater freedom in the Eastern European countries.

Gorbachev's change of policy quickly led to revolutions against Communist rule across Eastern Europe. The destruction of the Berlin Wall, which began on 9 November 1989, symbolised the end of Soviet control of Eastern Europe.

Impact on nationalism

The revolutions in Eastern Europe clearly had implications for the Soviet Republics. Across Eastern Europe countries had regained their independence from the USSR. Nationalists in the non-Russian Republics hoped that they could do the same.

Democratisation

Democratisation allowed nationalist groups to organise, win elections and assert their desire for independence. Nationalists gained majorities in several of the Republic's parliaments in the elections of 1990. These elections led to the first major nationalist challenge to the USSR.

- In March 1990 the newly elected Parliament of Lithuania declared Lithuanian independence from the USSR. Gorbachev claimed that the declaration was illegal and imposed economic sanctions. Although the sanctions were lifted in the summer, there was no resolution to the issue.

- In May 1990, Yeltsin took this process further by insisting that laws made by the Russian parliament were legally superior to Soviet laws. In effect, Yeltsin's statement gave Russia a significant degree of independence from the USSR.

The fight for Baltic independence

Nationalist movements, known as 'popular fronts', demanding Baltic independence gained influence from the late 1980s.

Estonian nationalism

Estonia declared itself sovereign, and therefore effectively independent of the USSR, in November 1988. Estonia did not leave the Union, but the government claimed the right to revive the old flag and begin education for citizens in the Estonian language.

Lithuanian nationalism

Lithuania's declaration of independence, in March 1990, came after nationalist victories in the election of a new Lithuanian Supreme Soviet. Gorbachev refused to accept the declaration. However, criticisms of the Tbilisi Massacre meant that Gorbachev was only prepared to use force against nationalists in the Baltic in extreme circumstances. Therefore, Gorbachev imposed economic sanctions, rather than using force. Sanctions failed to force Lithuania to accept Soviet rule. Therefore, in January 1991 the Soviet government sent in troops. Soviet forces occupied the press and television headquarters, killing 14 people.

Response to the killings

There was outrage at the use of force across the USSR.
- Ukrainian miners in Donetsk organised protests at the government's action.
- Yeltsin also asked Russian soldiers to refuse to obey any orders from the Soviet government that would suppress political protest. Yeltsin also started creating a Russian Army to defend the Russian Republic from Soviet attack.

Establish criteria

Below is a sample Section C exam question, which requires you to make a judgement. The key term in the question has been underlined. Defining the meaning of the key term can help you establish criteria that you can use to make a judgement.

Read the question, define the key term and then set out two or three criteria based on the key term, which you can use to reach and justify a judgement.

Study Extracts 1 and 2. In the light of differing interpretations, how convincing do you find the view that the USSR fell because of the <u>fundamental problems</u> created by Gorbachev's policies?

Definition

_____

Criteria to judge the extent to which fundamental problems created by Gorbachev's policies led to the fall of the USSR:

1
_____

2
_____

3
_____

Historians have different views about the reasons for the fall of the Soviet Union. Analyse and evaluate the extracts and use your knowledge of the issues to explain your answer to the following question. How far do you agree with the view that the collapse of the Soviet Union came about because of the failure of Gorbachev's policies? **AS**

EXTRACT 1

From Alec Nove, *An Economic History of the USSR 1917–1991*, published in 1993

By the summer of 1991 the process of disintegration was proceeding at an accelerated pace. Gorbachev's government had now neither money nor authority. Looking back, one is struck by a fundamental problem. To carry through the fundamental *perestroika* of the economy required strong government. In the first three years of Gorbachev's rule the mechanism for imposing a policy did exist. So Gorbachev set about dismantling the apparatus, changing its personnel, allowing criticism of the privileges, putting the whole system into question. *Glasnost* and *democratisation* undermined the power to implement policy. So by the time the reform programme was radicalized, the means to enforce it no longer existed. This, as well as doubts and hesitations about how far and how fast the reform process should go, plus the disastrous economic policy led to failure. Add the forces of nationalism and regionalism, and one had collapse.

EXTRACT 2

Robert Hornsby, *The Impact of the Nationalist Resurgence*, published in 2015

One of the key factors that quickly made nationalism a powerful force almost everywhere in the late 1980s was that so many leaders and elites in the different parts of the Soviet Union – most famously, Boris Yeltsin in Russia – decided that their ultimate allegiance was not to the Soviet Union but to their own republic, be that Russia, Ukraine, Georgia or anywhere else. Some surely made this decision based on genuine consideration of what was in the best interests of the people, others did so more cynically: with an eye on how best to protect their privileges and status in a post-Soviet world.

No single factor caused the collapse of the Soviet Union. What made nationalism so significant, though, was the unique way in which it was fed from virtually every direction: by economic decline, by limitations on religion and culture, by both political reform and political retrenchment, by local and national problems, and by the popular mood among the masses and the manoeuvring of local elites. One only needs to look today at the fifteen countries that emerged from the Soviet collapse as independent states to see that holding them all together under one umbrella was a virtual impossibility without the use of force.

The coup and the triumph of nationalism

Gorbachev responded to the growth of nationalism within the USSR by proposing reforms to the USSR which would allow the Republics more autonomy. However, treaty negotiations led to a coup, and the coup accelerated the disintegration of the USSR.

Treaty negotiations

Gorbachev proposed a new treaty to create a more decentralised union in 1990. Negotiations for a new treaty continued into 1991. By mid-July a complete draft of the treaty establishing a Union of Sovereign States had been agreed by the leaders of eight of the Soviet Republics. Gorbachev announced that the treaty would be signed on 21 August.

Response of hardliners

Hardliners within the Party believed that the new treaty would effectively end the USSR. Therefore, hardliners began plotting to bring down Gorbachev.

The coup

On 18 August, eight senior Communists announced the establishment of an Emergency Committee, which would replace Gorbachev's government. The Emergency Committee was led by Gorbachev's deputy, the head of the Army and the head of the KGB.

Yeltsin headed resistance to the coup. Army units were sent to the White House, the Russian parliament building, to arrest Yeltsin. However, the soldiers refused to obey orders and Yeltsin demanded Gorbachev's return to power.

Without the support of the army the Emergency Committee could not continue, and the coup collapsed on 21 August.

Break-up of the USSR

The failure of the coup precipitated the break-up of the USSR.

- Yeltsin's authority was strengthened by his response to the coup. Yeltsin used his new authority to attack the Communist Party. On 23 August Yeltsin suspended the Communist Party in Russia. As there was little popular opposition, Yeltsin went further and banned the Party on 6 November.

- Gorbachev's authority was weakened. After the coup, he reaffirmed his faith in the Communist Party. The majority of Soviet citizens wanted to end Communist rule; therefore they lost faith in Gorbachev.
- Fear that the Communist Party would reverse Gorbachev's reforms led nationalists in the Republics of Ukraine, Moldova, Azerbaijan, Kyrgyzstan and Armenia to declare their independence by early September.

The coup led to a series of fundamental changes. In essence, it finally destroyed the authority of Gorbachev and the Communist Party, the forces that had held the USSR together.

Independence

Gorbachev continued to try to save the USSR through negotiations with the leaders of the Republics. However, on 1 December 1991, 90 per cent of the people of Ukraine voted for independence from the USSR. Ukraine had the second-largest population of any of the Soviet Republics, containing almost 20 per cent of the Soviet population. Therefore, the Ukrainian decision to leave the USSR effectively ended Gorbachev's plan to save the Union.

As the USSR disintegrated Yeltsin and the leaders of Belarus and Ukraine signed the Minsk Agreement, which stated that the USSR had been replaced by the Commonwealth of Independent States (CIS). Eleven of the 15 former Soviet Republics joined the CIS on 21 December 1991.

The end of the USSR

The Minsk Agreement effectively destroyed the USSR. Gorbachev formally resigned as President of the USSR four days after the creation of the CIS and declared that the USSR would formally cease to exist on 31 December.

Linking extracts

Below are a sample Section C exam question and the two extracts to which it refers. In one colour, draw links between the extracts to show ways in which they agree about the fall of the Soviet Union. In another colour, draw links between the sources to show ways in which they disagree.

Study Extracts 1 and 2. In the light of differing interpretations, how convincing do you find the view that the USSR fell because of Gorbachev's failure to 'reconcile the results of Glasnost with the rise of the national question' (Extract 1)?

Historians have different views about the reasons for the fall of the Soviet Union. Analyse and evaluate the extracts and use your knowledge of the issues to explain your answer to the following question. How far do you agree with the view that the collapse of the Soviet Union came about because of the rise of nationalist movements? **AS**

EXTRACT 1

From David R. Marples, *The Collapse of the Soviet Union, 1985–1991*, published in 2004

Gorbachev's most important failure was not to reconcile the results of Glasnost with the rise of the national question in the Soviet Union. Problems in the republics surfaced almost immediately upon his taking office and were only exacerbated by the more tolerant atmosphere within the media. In the Baltic States, there were widespread protests. Arguably, Gorbachev could have negotiated the departure of the three Baltic States from the USSR and still maintained the Union. His hesitation ensured that the initiatives of the Baltic leaders, and particularly the Popular Fronts, filtered down to the other republics.

The rise in national sentiment in the republics received a significant boost from the downfall of Communist regimes in Eastern Europe. In the first instance, Gorbachev's abandonment of the Brezhnev Doctrine led to the overthrow of decrepit governments in Poland and East Germany which had almost no popular support. When the Soviet Union did not respond to stop the fall of Communism in Eastern Europe the Soviet republics could act with more confidence.

EXTRACT 2

From Mark Galeotti, *Gorbachev and His Revolution*, published in 1997

Gorbachev's economic strategy had been counter-productive and ruinous. He cut back on the central bureaucracy which had previously co-ordinated the economy, but without creating the sort of national market which could take its place. He wanted high technology industry, but with the budget deficit running at 35 billion rubles, he could not afford to pay for new plant or training.

There was a lack of any clear direction to economic reform. Instead, a series of short-sighted and often contradictory measures only continued to worsen matters. The failure of the economic side to *perestroika* inevitably had implications for the social aspects of reform. By the beginning of 1988, it was becoming clear to Gorbachev and his closest allies that they could not expect any imminent improvement in the economy. In fact, it was to prove on the verge of complete collapse. This was both a cause and an effect of their political problems. So long as reform seemed to be failing, then their position within the leadership only deteriorated. Without a strong mandate for change, though, they could never bring about the sort of dramatic reforms which might have had a chance of saving the USSR. This was another pivotal moment in Gorbachev's era, and one in which he took another important step away from his earlier, limited notions of reform towards a genuine revolution in Soviet politics.

Gorbachev's policies and the collapse of the USSR

Many historians argue that Gorbachev played a key role in the collapse of the USSR. Indeed, historian Archie Brown claims that the 'Gorbachev factor' was crucial to the USSR's fall.

Gorbachev's goals

Gorbachev's goals were radically different from the Soviet leaders of the period 1964-85. His goals changed over time:
- Initially, he proposed economic reform.
- In the late 1980s he embraced political reform.
- In 1990 he tried to reform to the nature of the Union.

Gorbachev's reforms

Historians have argued that Gorbachev's various reforms, and their failure, caused the collapse of the USSR.

New thinking

Gorbachev's reforms were underpinned by what Gorbachev called 'new thinking'. New thinking was based on a new language of politics, which undermined the USSR.
- 'Perestroika': Gorbachev used the term because it implied scientific restructuring. He did not use the word 'reform' because it was associated with Khrushchev's failures. Nonetheless, the new term allowed him to advocate change.
- 'Socialist pluralism', 'socialist markets': traditionally Communists had rejected 'pluralism' and 'markets', which they associated with capitalism. By adding the word 'socialist', Gorbachev suggested that markets and pluralism were compatible with Communism.

New leadership

Gorbachev's decision to replace local leaders in the Republics with his supporters from Russia weakened the authority of the Communist Party. Soviet citizens in the Republics outside Russia saw this as a Russian takeover, and responded by supporting nationalist leaders.

Perestroika

Gorbachev described his reforms as *Perestroika* – restructuring. *Perestroika* went through a series of phases, each of which weakened the party and the Union.
- Acceleration (1985–86) led to a decline in economic growth, making economic conditions worse and undermining faith in the Party. The failure of these reforms also led Gorbachev to initiate more radical economic and political reforms.

- Glasnost exposed the crimes of previous Soviet governments. Consequently, it undermined faith not only in the Communist Party but in the ideology on which it was based. In this sense, glasnost led to a more profound loss of faith in the system than rationalisation.
- Democratisation weakened the Communist Party by allowing alternative candidates to stand. It also weakened Gorbachev's control of the Party, as Soviet voters chose their candidates. Therefore, the Party no longer had a monopoly of patronage.
- Market reform weakened the Communist Party, as it further destabilised the economy and was a tacit admission that the command economy was inferior to Western capitalism.

Renouncing violence

Gorbachev also renounced violence as a method for holding together both the USSR and the Eastern Bloc. Traditionally, Soviet leaders had relied on violence to deal with opposition. Although the Soviet authorities still used violence in some cases, Gorbachev reduced the emphasis on violence and in so doing weakened the Party's ability to hold the Union together.

Embracing rights

Traditionally, Soviet leaders had argued that individual rights, such as the right to free speech, were part of capitalist ideology, and therefore of no value in a Communist country. Gorbachev, however, argued that the government needed to respect individual rights in order to ensure that there was no repeat of Stalin's atrocities.

Gorbachev's commitment to individual rights played a key role in the fall of the USSR because it weakened the power of the Party to repress opposition.

The consequences of Gorbachev's reforms

Ultimately, Gorbachev's reforms failed to revive and renew the USSR. Rather, they led to economic chaos and a decline in faith in the Communist Party and the USSR.

Add own knowledge

Read the following question and the accompanying extracts. Then add detail from your own knowledge around the edges of both extracts. Draw links between the extracts and the details showing how they support or challenge the interpretations offered by the extracts. You can add knowledge that supports *and challenges* the extract. You can also add new alternative arguments that challenge the interpretation offered by the extract.

In the light of differing interpretations, how convincing do you find the view that 'the Soviet collapse was also due in great measure to the policy choices made by Gorbachev' (Extract 1)?

Study Extracts 1 and 2. Historians have different views about the reasons for the fall of the Soviet Union. Analyse and evaluate the extracts and use your knowledge of the issues to explain your answer to the following question. How far do you agree with the view that the collapse of the Soviet Union came about because of Gorbachev's mistakes? **AS**

EXTRACT 1

From Christopher Marsh, *Unparalleled Reforms: China's Rise, Russia's Fall and the Interdependence of Transition*, published in 2005

While the collapse of the Soviet Union was not inevitable prior to the launching of *perestroika*, it became increasingly likely as events unfolded and decisions were made about how to proceed. The first real phase of the collapse began between March and December 1989, from the initial elections to the Congress of People's Deputies to the collapse of Communist rule in Eastern Europe. By this time *perestroika* had run into trouble. Gorbachev attempted to reinvigorate his reform agenda by pushing ahead with democratisation. But in so doing Gorbachev gave the vote to a population largely in need of food.

During the second phase of collapse, from January 1900 to August 1991, collapse of the system became an increasingly possible outcome of reform. Yeltsin's meteoric rise to power in Russia, and his call to the republics to swallow as much sovereignty as they could was a lethal blow to the Soviet Union. The failure of the coup led the country into the final phase of collapse, which saw the Soviet Union crumple piece by piece throughout the autumn of 1991.

While long term conditions certainly contributed to the failure of Communism, the Soviet collapse was also due in great measure to the policy choices made by Gorbachev, particularly in regard to the pace and scope of reform.

EXTRACT 2

From Mark R. Beissinger, *Nationalism and the Collapse of Soviet Communism*, published in 2009

Gorbachev's policy of glasnost and the political liberalisation that it produced were obviously the critical institutional conditions that allowed the collapse of communism to occur. Without glasnost, the forces that most directly brought about the collapse could never have materialised or been able to act. But despite the absolute importance of the Gorbachev factor and the broader factors that led Gorbachev to choose this path, we should also remember that the collapse of communism was in fact the unintended result of Gorbachev s policies, not its conscious goal, and that the collapse occurred precisely because other social forces moved into the widening political space that glasnost afforded.

The issues that effectively mobilised populations within the Soviet Union during these years revolved precisely around nationalism. To be sure, issues of democratisation, labour unrest and consumer shortages, and environmental justice constituted autonomous vectors of mobilisation, at times intersecting with nationalism and at times diverging from it. But as my own study of thousands of protest demonstrations throughout the Soviet Union during the glasnost period showed, nationalism gained a particular force and appeal not enjoyed by these other movements.

Gorbachev's failures and the collapse of the USSR

REVISED

Some historians emphasise Gorbachev's failures in the collapse of the USSR.

Gorbachev's fundamental mistakes

Some historians argue that Gorbachev made fundamental mistakes that led to the collapse of the USSR. They argue that:

- Gorbachev's fundamental mistake was believing that reform could save the USSR.
- Gorbachev failed to anticipate the effects of glasnost or the extent to which revelations about the past would undermine the claims of the Communist Party.
- He failed to see the fragility of commitment to the USSR. In this sense, he believed the Communist Party's own propaganda that Communism had created a new Soviet people who no longer felt the pull of nationalism.
- Gorbachev's reforms created the crisis that destroyed the USSR. Without them the USSR could have continued for decades.

Gorbachev's policy mistakes

Some historians argue that Gorbachev made key policy mistakes that led to the collapse of the USSR.

- His initial policy of *uskoreniye* was designed to restructure industry *and* increase output. Restructuring would disrupt production, thus lowering output in the short term. Increasing production would make it impossible to restructure. These competing objectives are one reason why the policy failed.
- He continually introduced new reforms. His constant changes of direction meant that his policies never had the time they needed to succeed.
- Gorbachev attempted economic and political reform at the same time, and therefore he weakened the entire Soviet system.
- Gorbachev continually weakened the power of the Party, but did not establish a new powerbase with the authority to hold the USSR together.

Gorbachev's tactical mistakes

Some historians argue that Gorbachev's tactical mistakes explain the collapse of the USSR. They argue that:

- Gorbachev failed to win over the Communist Party. The Party was the only institution that was strong enough to introduce reform. However, in practice the Party resisted reform, and therefore hampered Gorbachev's programme.

- Having embraced democracy he refused to stand for election, weakening his own position.
- Having survived the coup, he failed to abandon the Communist Party, and therefore he lost public support.

Contrast with China

Some historians contrast Gorbachev's failed reforms with China's successful reforms. At the beginning of the 1980s, China was a Communist country with many of the same features as the USSR. Chinese leaders introduced reforms, and yet the Communist Party of China retained power. Some historians argue that the Chinese reforms show that Gorbachev could have succeeded in reforming the USSR and retained Communist control. They argue:

- Chinese Communists embraced market reform more quickly and comprehensively than Gorbachev. As a result, China's economy continued to grow during the process of reform. Therefore, the Communist Party retained its political authority. By contrast, Gorbachev's economic reforms were slow and inconsistent. Gorbachev mistakenly tried to integrate markets into a command economy. This approach failed, creating an economic crisis, which led to widespread dissatisfaction with the Soviet Communist Party.
- Communist leaders in China introduced economic reform without allowing political freedom. The lack of political reform meant that China continued to be politically stable during the reform process. From this perspective, the USSR collapsed because Gorbachev tried to introduce economic and political reform at the same time. Therefore, when *perestroika* led to economic chaos, the Soviet people were able to protest and vote for new leaders, which led to the break-up of the USSR.

Conclusion

Gorbachev's mistakes, and his inability to foresee the consequences of his policies undermined the authority of the Communist Party and his own position. Therefore, by 1991 it was impossible for either Gorbachev or the Communist Party to hold the Union together.

Highlighting integration

Below are a sample A Level Section C exam question and two paragraphs written in answer. Read the question, the two answers and the extracts. Then highlight examples of integration – where extracts are used together. Which paragraph best integrates the extracts in order to answer the question?

In the light of differing interpretations, how convincing do you find the view that the USSR fell because of 'a failure of Gorbachev's triple revolution'? (Extract 1).

In conclusion, the view that the USSR fell because of a failure of Gorbachev's 'triple revolution' (Extract 1) is broadly convincing because perestroika destabilised the Soviet Union by introducing economic and political reforms. In so doing, as Extract 1 argues, it caused economic chaos and then democratised the system allowing the Soviet people to reject the Communist Party and the Soviet Union. Moreover, Yeltsin 'played a vital role in defeating the right-wing forces behind the August 1991' (Extract 2). However, Yeltsin was only able to play this important role because of the freedoms Gorbachev had introduced. Therefore, while Yeltsin played an important role in the last phase of collapse, and while there were clearly long-term issues (Extract 1), the pace and scope of Gorbachev's reforms were crucial to the Soviet collapse because having destabilised the economy he introduced political freedoms and therefore allowed Soviet citizens to reject Communism and the Soviet Union.

Extract 1 clearly argues that the USSR fell because of 'a failure of Gorbachev's triple revolution'. From this point of view, Gorbachev's three revolutions led to economic collapse and a growth of nationalism – that led to a break-up in the union. In this sense, it was Gorbachev's decision to reform all three aspects at speed that led to collapse. Extract 2 puts a very different argument. Sakwa argues that Yeltsin's reaction to the August coup was the main cause of the Soviet Union's collapse. The coup, the extract argues, allowed Yeltsin to create a 'revolution.' Clearly, there is truth in both extracts.

EXTRACT 1

From Ronald Grigor Suny, *The Revenge of the Past*, published in 1993

The death of the Soviet Union represented a failure of Gorbachev's triple revolution. The system fell because the leadership tried simultaneously to dismantle the old practices of the command economy and Communist Party dominance to construct a democratic multinational federation. Nations formed within the USSR tore that superpower into fragments, each with its competing interests and aspirations, and Gorbachev's program fell victim to the economic collapse and the rise of powerful nationalism. Once it became possible to break the imperial tie with Russia, nationalist leaders moved to take control of the destinies of their own peoples.

The forces of nationalism, which undermined the former Soviet Union and Gorbachev's plans for gradual economic and political reform initiated from above, were an understandable reaction to the hyper-centralism and bureaucratization of the old system.

EXTRACT 2

From Richard Sakwa, *Russian Politics and Society*, published in 2008

The attempted coup of August 1991 sought to resolve by forceful means the crisis of power and end the struggle of conflicting ideologies. Yeltsin transformed the coup into a revolution. At a session of the Russian parliament the next day the CPSU was suspended in Russia by a stroke of Yeltsin's pen. The retreat of the Party turned into a rout. On 24 August Gorbachev resigned as General Secretary of the CPSU and called for the dissolution of the Central Committee. On 29 August the USSR Supreme Soviet suspended the CPSU, and on 6 November 1991 Yeltsin banned the Party in Russia.

The attempt by conservatives to halt the tide of disintegration by staging a coup only accelerated the demise of the old system and the state. The coup was the final act of one of the cruellest regimes in human history.

Yeltsin and the collapse of the USSR

While some historians argue that Gorbachev played the key role in the fall of the USSR, others argue that Yeltsin was the primary cause of its collapse.

Yeltsin, like Gorbachev, was a member of the Communist Party under Brezhnev. Initially, Yeltsin supported Gorbachev. However, by the late 1980s he became critical of Gorbachev's unwillingness to embrace wholesale political and economic reform.

Popular radical

Yeltsin emerged as a popular radical at the very time when Gorbachev was becoming increasingly unpopular and conservative.

- Yeltsin had a reputation for attacking the corruption and the privileges of the Communist Party.
- He publicly attacked Communists who opposed reform.
- He campaigned in the 1989 elections for radical reform, and won 89 per cent of the vote in Moscow.
- Following his victory in the 1989 election, he used his democratic mandate to criticise Gorbachev and the Communist Party.
- He helped form the IRDG (see page 74). In this sense, he formed an organised opposition group within the Congress of People's Deputies.

Yeltsin and the Party

Yeltsin damaged the authority of the Party by resigning from the Communist Party in July 1990. Yeltsin had been a popular member of the Party, and therefore when he left the Party's popularity declined. Indeed, Yeltsin's resignation was part of a mass exodus from the Party: during 1990 Party membership dropped from 19.2 million members to 16.5 million. Party popularity also dropped to a mere 18.8 per cent.

Gorbachev's rival

By 1990 Yeltsin was Gorbachev's most high-profile and popular opponent. In June 1990 opinion polls showed that Yeltsin was more popular than Gorbachev among Russian voters.

Not only did Yeltsin set out a rival and more radical programme to Gorbachev, Yeltsin presented himself as a rival leader, who could lead a non-Communist government.

Yeltsin and nationalism

Yeltsin was also significant because he advocated nationalism. By emphasising the rights and autonomy of Russia, Yeltsin weakened the USSR.

Yeltsin also supported the growth of nationalism in other Soviet Republics. During the summer of 1990 he visited several Soviet Republics advising their leaders to 'take as much sovereignty as you can swallow.' In 1991 Yeltsin supported the Baltic states' declarations of independence from the USSR. In so doing, he supported the creation of national governments, which rivalled and undermined the power of the USSR.

Rival powerbase

Gorbachev consistently weakened his own powerbase. Yeltsin, by contrast, established a new powerbase through winning elections to the Russian Parliament and the Russian Presidency.

Yeltsin had democratic legitimacy as he had been elected. Gorbachev had never stood for election, and therefore the Soviet people increasingly believed that Gorbachev's power was illegitimate.

Yeltsin and the coup

Yeltsin also played a significant role in the destruction of the USSR due to his handling of the coup.

- Yeltsin became the centre of opposition to the coup.
- He used the coup as a pretext to ban the Communist Party in Russia.
- He seized Communist Party assets, undermining the Party's ability to control the Union.
- Yeltsin emerged from the coup as a hero, whereas Gorbachev's reputation was further damaged.

Yeltsin and the Union

Following the coup, Yeltsin organised a secret meeting with the leaders of Ukraine and Belarus. The three leaders agreed to destroy Gorbachev's new Union Treaty by forming the CIS.

Following the meeting, he persuaded the leaders of the Soviet military to abandon the USSR and form the new Russian Army. Without an army Gorbachev had no way of holding the Union together.

Conclusion

Clearly Yeltsin played a key role in the last phase of the collapse of the USSR. But there is considerable debate over the extent to which he, rather than Gorbachev, caused the collapse of the Union.

Write the question

The following extracts relate to the causes of the collapse of the Soviet Union. Having read the previous pages about the Soviet Union's collapse write a Section C exam-style question to accompany the extracts.

Study Extracts 1 and 2. In the light of differing interpretations, how convincing do you find the view that

_____

_____

To explain your answer, analyse and evaluate the material in both extracts, using your own knowledge of the issues.

Study Extracts 1 and 2. Historians have different views about the reasons for the fall of the Soviet Union. Analyse and evaluate the extracts and use your knowledge of the issues to explain your answer to the following question. How far do you agree with the view that **AS**

_____

_____

EXTRACT 1

From Archie Brown, *The Soviet Union*, published in 2004

Gorbachev faced intense pressures from different directions from conservative communists occupying strong positions in the party apparatus; from national elites demanding, in some cases, separate statehood; and from a highly politicized Russian society now able to voice its discontent at the persistence of economic shortages and social problems.

The breakup of the Soviet Union into fifteen states was facilitated by the new freedom and political pluralism that Gorbachev played the major role in introducing in the second half of the 1980s. Yet that disintegration of the state was the ultimate unintended consequence of his actions. The more immediate causes of the breakup were, however, Yeltsin's playing of the Russian nationalist card against the Union and the intervention of the putschists who took their action when they did to prevent the signing of the agreed Union Treaty (that devolved massive powers to the republics) and, in their folly, hastened what they had sought to prevent.

EXTRACT 2

From George W. Breslauer, *Gorbachev and Yeltsin as Leaders*, published in 2002

Yeltsin polarized politics during these last two to three years of Gorbachev's leadership. No matter what Gorbachev proposed in domestic policy, Yeltsin criticized the Party leader for conservatism and half-measures. He supported centrifugal forces in the union republics at a time when Gorbachev was trying to contain. He argued that the Soviet authorities were the main obstacle to Russia's achieving a decisive transition to a new political order. He initiated a 'war of laws', contesting or blocking the enforcement of Soviet laws on the territory of the Russian republic. He sponsored a declaration of Russian 'sovereignty' and supported other republics that were doing the same. Yeltsin, over time, became increasingly determined to destroy both Gorbachev's authority and the Kremlin's powers.

Yeltsin may not have decided until November–December *1991* to work behind the scenes to dissolve the Soviet Union. But it was increasingly clear by fall of 1991 that Gorbachev was finished as a serious political force and that the future of Russia would be shaped by the decisions of President Yeltsin.

Exam focus (A Level)

Below is a sample high-level A Level essay. Read the question and the accompanying extracts, as well as the essay and the comments around it.

In the light of differing interpretations, how convincing do you find the view that the collapse of the Soviet Union was brought about by Gorbachev's decision to 'seek popular support by introducing representative institutions'?

EXTRACT 1

From Lee Edwards, *The Collapse of Communism*, published in 2013

The Soviet economy in the 1980s was in deep trouble. The CIA forecast virtually zero growth, and even within the Soviet Union voices were heard calling for major changes in the way the economy was run. A heavy and unanticipated blow was the sudden drop in the price of oil, the country's leading export. The decline in earning from this source forced Moscow to resort to heavy borrowing abroad. Attempts to liberalize and rationalise the way the economy operated encountered staunch resistance from the bureaucracy, whose livelihood depended on the command economy. The bureaucracy's defiance impelled Gorbachev to seek popular support by introducing representative institutions. This had the effect of destroying the party's monopoly on political power – the essential feature of the regime instituted by Lenin, which soon brought the whole union down.

EXTRACT 2

From Archie Brown, *The Gorbachev Era*, published in 2006

Events conspired against the preservation of even a smaller union. The election of Yeltsin as Russian president in June 1991 gave him a legitimacy to speak for Russia that was now greater than that of Gorbachev, who had been only indirectly elected by a legislature representing the whole of the USSR more than a year earlier. For some time Yeltsin had been pressing for Russian sovereignty within the Union.

The putsch was, however, the mortal blow both for the Union and for the leadership of Gorbachev. Having seen how close they had been to being fully reincorporated in a Soviet state which would have been a throwback to the past, the Baltic states instantly declared their independence. While Gorbachev had been isolated on the Crimean coast, Yeltsin had been the public face of resistance to the coup, and Gorbachev's position became weaker and Yeltsin's stronger in its aftermath.

Extract 1 clearly argues that Gorbachev's decision to 'seek popular support by introducing representative institutions' was the key trigger for the collapse of the Soviet Union. However, Extract 2 claims that it was the August coup, or 'putsch', that was the 'mortal blow ... for the Union'. Significantly, both of these arguments relate to the idea of representation and legitimacy, as Extract 2 implies that one of the reasons for the decline of Gorbachev's authority compared to Yeltsin was that he could not claim to represent the people in the way that Yeltsin did during and after the coup. In this sense, representation was crucial to the failure of the Union, as by the time of the coup Gorbachev's reforms had linked representation to the right to rule. Finally, it is also important to note the significance of the Soviet Union's economic problems, mentioned in Extract 1, and nationalism, which is discussed in Extract 2.

The essay opens by demonstrating a clear understanding of the extracts.

The introduction contains an initial analysis of the issues raised in the extracts, and shows an understanding of the basis of the arguments of both extracts.

Gorbachev's decision to 'seek popular support by introducing representative institutions' was the most important cause of the Soviet Union's collapse, as Extract 1 claims. The introduction of representative institutions was part of a series of political reforms that Gorbachev introduced after becoming leader of the Communist Party (CP) in 1985. Gorbachev's first major political reforms, known as glasnost, included the liberalisation of the media and public acknowledgements of the problems that the Soviet Union was facing. However, glasnost, and Gorbachev's economic policies, faced opposition from within the CP. Indeed, as Extract 1 argues it was 'the bureaucracy's defiance' of his initiative that led Gorbachev to introduce representative institutions, because Gorbachev used them to 'seek popular support' for his reforms. In 1988 Gorbachev revived the soviets by allowing multi-candidate elections, which Gorbachev hoped would lead to the victory of reformers. The 1989 and 1990 elections took this process further. However, rather than strengthen Gorbachev's position, by 1990 they had undermined it. Gorbachev's democratisation had created elected representatives who had authority straight from the people, which neither he nor the CP could claim. This, as Extract 1 argues, had the 'effect of destroying the party's monopoly on political power' because the Party's authority was eclipsed by the new representatives who had been elected by the people.

> The essay integrates issues raised by the extracts with those from own knowledge.

> The paragraph presents an evaluative argument.

Extract 2 puts forward an alternative interpretation. It argues that the coup destroyed Gorbachev and the Soviet Union. The coup, it argues, allowed Yeltsin to emerge as the leader of Russia, while Gorbachev's authority was damaged. Significantly, Extract 2 acknowledges that Yeltsin's election as Russian President in 1991, 'gave him a legitimacy to speak for Russia that was now greater than that of Gorbachev'. This recognises the significance of representative institutions, and the way in which they robbed the CP of its authority. In this way, Extract 2, in part at least, supports the view that it was the combination of Gorbachev's appeal to the people combined with his creation of the Russian Presidency that undermined the Soviet Union because these reforms acknowledged the principle of elected authority.

> The paragraph begins by interpreting the extracts with confidence and discrimination, analysing the issues raised.

Extract 2, however, also indicates that nationalism played a role in the downfall of the Soviet Union. Indeed, it argues that Yeltsin's authority increased not simply because he was elected but because he became 'the public face of resistance to the coup'. This is undoubtedly true. While Gorbachev had been pushing for reform in the mid-1980s, by the early 1990s Gorbachev had become more cautious, and Yeltsin had emerged as the leader of radical reformers. This was particularly clear in terms of nationalism, as 'Yeltsin had been pressing for Russian sovereignty' for some time prior to the coup, and had defended the right to self-determination of other Soviet Republics. However, Extract 2 misses the point that the rise of nationalism was encouraged by the representative institutions that Gorbachev founded. The national elections of 1990 were a turning point in terms of Gorbachev's authority, because they created legitimate local leaders across the Soviet Union who could appeal to nationalism and in so doing undermine the Soviet Union.

> Integrates issues raised by extracts with those from own knowledge when discussing the presented evidence and differing arguments.

The economy, as implied by Extract I, also played a role. As Extract I argues, 'The Soviet economy ... was in deep trouble'. The Soviet economy had many problems. Between 1965 and 1985 the proportion of GDP spent on defence increased from around 12 per cent to 17 per cent. This starved the economy of funds to invest. Also, as Extract I shows, the 'sudden drop in the price of oil' caused even greater problems as oil was 'the country's leading export'. Extract I does not, however, acknowledge the impact on the authority of the CP. Since the 1930s the CP had claimed authority to govern based on the success of its economic policies. However, by the late 1980s the Soviet Union was experiencing an economic crisis. Therefore, at the very moment that Gorbachev's reforms were giving authority to elected representatives, the Party's traditional source of authority was declining because it had clearly failed to stop the economic crisis.

Extract I is correct to argue that Gorbachev's decision to appeal to the people by creating representative institutions was the key reason for the fall of the Soviet Union. In essence, this introduced the principle that representative government was legitimate in a way that the CP simply was not. By 1990 this had led to the emergence of a new generation of leaders who represented the different nations of the Soviet Union, including Yeltsin, who represented Russia, the biggest of the Republics. The economic crisis and the coup finally destroyed the authority of the CP meaning that elected representatives could oust it, and break up the union that the CP had held together since the end of the Civil War.

> The conclusion finishes the sustained evaluative argument developed across the essay.

This essay achieves a mark in Level 5 as it interprets both extracts with confidence, and clearly understands the basis of the interpretations offered by both extracts. It also integrates issues raised by the extracts with those from own knowledge and presents a sustained evaluative argument, reaching a fully substantiated judgement on the interpretations of both extracts.

Reverse engineering

The best essays are based on careful plans. Read the essay and the examiner's comments and try to work out the general points of the plan used to write the essay. Also, look at how the two extracts are used in the answer. Once you have done this, note down the specific examples used to support each general point.

Exam focus (AS Level)

Below is a sample high-level AS Level essay. Read the question and the accompanying extracts, as well as the essay and the comments around it.

Historians have different views about the reasons for the fall of the Soviet Union. Analyse and evaluate the extracts and use your knowledge of the issues to explain your answer to the following question.

How far do you agree with the view that 'the USSR disintegrated due to its economic weaknesses'?

EXTRACT 1

From Robin Bunce, *Communist States in the Twentieth Century*, published in 2015

Between 1985 and 1991 there was a fundamental shift in global politics. A series of profound changes, including the disintegration of the Eastern Bloc, the fall of the Berlin Wall and the end of the Cold War, climaxed with the fall of the Soviet Union.

Some historians argue that the USSR disintegrated due to its economic weaknesses. From this point of view the collapse of the USSR had roots in the late 1920s. Stalin's decision to collectivise agriculture and introduce a command economy created an economic system that was fundamentally inefficient. According to this perspective, free markets would always outperform command economies in the long run. This became increasingly apparent in the late 1950s. Under Khrushchev the economy declined, under Brezhnev it stagnated, and finally under Gorbachev it collapsed. Some historians link this to the arms race. They argue that the USSR's economic weaknesses were exacerbated by massive defence spending, which meant that other areas of the economy were starved of money. Economic collapse, in turn, caused political collapse.

EXTRACT 2

From Ronald Grigor Suny, *The Revenge of the Past: Nationalism, Revolution, and the Collapse of the Soviet Union*, published in 1993

When Gorbachev came to power in March 1985, the Soviet state was already in a profoundly weakened condition. The Soviet Union had experienced not only years of political and economic stagnation but also a frustrating absence of able and stable leadership in the first half of the 1980s. Weakness in the centre had enabled the local ethnic and regional mafias within the Party-state apparatus to increase their power. In nearly every Transcaucasian and Central Asian republic a series of purges (1985–1988) eliminated the top leaders and brought demonstrators onto the streets.

When these 'democratic' forces began to act, the emergence of nationalist politics burst the bounds of the old politics in a number of republics. In a number of republics – Armenia, Georgia, the Baltic states – this rapidly undermined the power of local Communist parties. In other republics, however – in Central Asia most particularly – *perestroika* was contained and Communist apparatchiks maintained their hold on both state and society.

Extract 1 and Extract 2 offer different interpretations of why the Soviet Union collapsed in 1991. Extract 1 argues that 'the USSR disintegrated due to its economic weaknesses', linking the long-term economic weaknesses to the issue of the 'arms race'. Extract 2 gives a different interpretation. First, it points to 'political and economic stagnation'. However, it also argues that '"democratic" forces' in the Soviet Republics also played a role. Extract 1 is right that economic weaknesses played a role. However, economic decline did not threaten the long-term survival of the Soviet Union until Gorbachev's economic and political reforms created a crisis.

> The essay opens with a strong focus on the interpretations offered by the extracts.

> This paragraph focuses clearly on the key issue raised in the question.

Extract 1 argues that 'Economic collapse ... caused political collapse'. Extract 1 focuses on long-term problems with the Soviet economy. It argues, 'free markets would always outperform command economies in the long run', noting that by the 1970s this was becoming increasingly clear. The Soviet command economy had a series of weaknesses. It was wasteful, labour productivity was low, and there were few incentives to innovate or improve. These problems were features of the system. Stalin had designed a situation that prioritised the production of large quantities of raw materials over quality of production or the production of sophisticated goods. As the economy provided few consumer goods there were no incentives to work hard. Extract 2 recognises these long-term problems arguing that even in 1985 'the Soviet state was already in a profoundly weakened condition'. Gorbachev's reforms, however, made the situation worse. Gorbachev's anti-alcohol campaign further limited the availability of consumer goods and cut state tax revenues by 67 billion roubles, the equivalent of 9 per cent of GDP. Gorbachev's market reforms undermined the central planning system, while failing to create an effective alternative for organising the economy. The result was economic chaos. Therefore, Extracts 1 and 2 are right: long-term economic stagnation was a problem, but perestroika undermined the Soviet Union by creating economic chaos.

> The essay considers the interpretation of both extracts.

> This paragraph uses both of the extracts to examine the extent to which economic problems led to the fall of the Soviet Union.

Extract 1 links Soviet economic problems to the arms race. It argues, 'the USSR's economic weaknesses were exacerbated by massive defence spending'. Spending on defence reached 17 per cent of GDP in 1985. This was much higher than US defence spending, which was just 6 per cent of GDP. As Extract 1 argues, this meant that 'other areas of the economy were starved of money'. As a result, Gorbachev was forced to borrow money from the West in order to invest in his 'acceleration', or *uskorenie*, programme. As a result, government debt rose from $18.1 billion in 1981 to $27.2 billion in 1988, which led to inflation. Clearly, as Extract 1 argues, the arms race made the economic situation in the USSR worse as it forced the government to borrow to invest, and this in turn created inflation.

> This paragraph uses detailed own knowledge to support the argument of Extract 1.

Extract 2 argues that there were significant political problems that weakened the Soviet Union. First it argues that the Soviet Union had suffered from a 'frustrating absence of able and stable leadership in the first half of the 1980s'. This is a reference to Brezhnev's last years and the rule of Andropov and Chernenko. During this period, there was little meaningful reform. However, Extract 2 may be overstating the problems that Andropov and Chernenko created. They did little to reform the system, but at the same time, they did not destabilise the system either. Gorbachev gave the Soviet Union better leadership but this created all kinds of problems. His economic reforms made the economy worse and his political reform exposed this, and allowed people to organise against Party rule.

Indeed, Extract 2 shows just how damaging Gorbachev's reforms were. Gorbachev's 'purges (1985–1988) eliminated the top leaders' in many of the Soviet Republics. Brezhnev had allowed local leaders to play a major role in Soviet politics. Gorbachev believed that these 'regional mafias' were corrupt, and therefore replaced them with Russians. The removal of 'local ethnic' leaders caused outrage in the Republics and 'brought demonstrators onto the streets'. Gorbachev's reforms made matters worse. Democratic elections gave power to nationalists in 'Armenia, Georgia, the Baltic'. Yeltsin was the most powerful of the new 'democratic forces'; even before the coup he was already undermining Gorbachev's authority by arguing that elected local leaders should have authority rather than the unelected Communist Party. In this sense, Extract 2 is right: nationalism was a key reason for the fall of the Soviet Union as it 'rapidly undermined the power of local Communist parties' across most of the Soviet Union with the exception of Central Asia.

Overall, Extract 1 is right that economic problems were a key part of the collapse of the Soviet Union. However, they were not the only reasons. Extract 1 focuses on the long-term economic issues. However, until 1985 the declining economy did not seem to threaten the long-term survival of the Soviet Union. It was Gorbachev's reforms that turned economic decline into economic chaos and it was Gorbachev's politics, as argued in Extract 2, which 'rapidly undermined the power of local Communist parties'. Therefore, Gorbachev's reforms were a more important reason than long-term economic problems because the reforms created the crisis that the Soviet Union could not survive.

> The conclusion reaches a clear and supported overall judgement.

This essay gets a mark in Level 4 as it analyses the interpretations of both extracts, integrating detailed own knowledge to reach a supported overall judgement.

Reverse engineering

The best essays are based on careful plans. Read the essay and the examiner's comments and try to work out the general points of the plan used to write the essay. Also, look at how the two extracts are used in the answer. Once you have done this, note down the specific examples used to support each general point.

Glossary

All-union   Relating to the entire Soviet Union.

Anticolonial   Dedicated to the overthrow of imperialism.

Arms race   A competition to develop and produce increasingly deadly weapons. During the Cold War the arms race focused on nuclear missiles.

Authoritarian   A form of government that has strict limits on individual freedom.

Autonomy   Self-government.

Black market   The illegal trading of goods and services.

Bourgeoisie   The term used by Karl Marx to describe the middle class.

Building socialism   The process of building a new, more equal economy and society.

Bureaucratic regime   A government that is dominated by administrative officials.

Cadres   Small groups of specially trained people. A term used to refer to Communist Party officials.

Capitalism   An economic system based on free trade and the private ownership of property.

Central Committee   The body within the Communist Party that was responsible for investigating and disciplining Party members who were accused of corruption.

Centralised   A political or economic system in which power and control is concentrated in one location.

Cheka   A political police force created by Lenin.

Cold War   A period of heightened political tension between the capitalist West, led by America, and the Communist East, led by Russia.

Consumer goods   Products that are designed to be used by individuals for their own benefit, such as shoes, refrigerators or cigarettes.

Cult of personality   An idealised image of a leader created by the media.

Decrees   Laws usually issued by the central government.

De-Stalinisation   The process of ending some of the policies introduced by and associated with Stalin.

Detente   Name given to the process of removal of tensions between the superpowers in the late 1960s and 1970s; features included arms limitations agreements and state visits.

Eastern Bloc   A term for the Communist states of central and eastern Europe, which were allied with the Soviet Union.

Factions   Groups of people within a political party who share a common set of beliefs and who are in opposition to the leadership of the party.

Free love   A social movement that rejected marriage.

General Secretary   The most senior administrator in the Communist Party. Over time, the role became increasingly important. By 1928 the General Secretary was effectively the leader of the Communist Party.

Gosplan   The organisation responsible for economic planning the Soviet economy.

Glasnost   Political reforms introduced by Gorbachev, which aimed to make Soviet politics more open.

Great Terror   The period from 1936 to 38 in which Stalin purged the Communist Party, the army and industry, resulting in around 10 million deaths.

Greens   This group fought against the Reds and the Whites during the Civil War. They drew support from peasants and their policies focused on redistributing land to the peasants.

House arrest   A form of imprisonment in which the prisoner is forced to stay in their own house.

Hyperinflation   An economic situation in which inflation increased dramatically, usually for a sustained period.

Kulaks   Rich peasants.

Labour productivity   A measure of the amount produced by workers in a specified period.

Leningrad   Russia's second city. It was known as Petrograd until 1924, when it was renamed Leningrad to commemorate Lenin's death. Since 1991 it has been known as St Petersburg.

Light industry   Manufacturing that produces consumer goods.

Minister of the Interior   The member of the government responsible for law and order within the Soviet Union.

Mixed economy   An economy in which the state and private enterprise both play a significant role.

Nationalisation   The process by which private property is taken over by the state.

New Economic Policy (NEP)   A semi-capitalist economic policy introduced by Lenin in 1921 to help revive Russia's economy after a famine.

Nobility   The traditional ruling class, also known as the aristocracy.

Nomenklatura   Administrators in the Communist Party of the Soviet government.

October Revolution   The Revolution in which the Bolshevik Party seized power in Russia.

Orthodox Church   Russia's traditional Church. Until 1918 the Church represented Russia's official religion.

Perestroika   Economic reforms introduced by Gorbachev, which were designed to restructure the Soviet economy.

Photomontage   An artistic technique in which photographs are collaged together.

Politburo   The most senior committee of the Communist Party.

Polytechnic   A type of education which teaches many practical skills.

Pragmatic   A policy which is designed to achieve specific results, rather than to reflect certain values. Pragmatic policies are often contrasted with idealistic policies.

Private ownership   The ownership of capital or property by private individuals or private companies.

Profiteering   Making money through illegal trade.

Pronatalist   Propaganda, policies and politicians that advocate childbirth.

Provisional Government   The government that ruled the Russian Empire on a temporary basis after the fall of the Tsar. The Provisional Government was deposed by Lenin's October Revolution.

Rabkrin   The Workers and Peasants Inspectorate. A body set up by Lenin to investigate allegations of corruption in the Communist Party. It had the power to discipline and sack members of the Communist Party.

Red Terror   A period from 1918 to 1921 in which the Communists used violence and intimidation to suppress their political opponents.

Rehabilitated   The process by which Communists who were considered criminals by Stalin were pardoned or found not guilty of their alleged crimes after Stalin's death.

Resolution   A proposal submitted to the Communist Party Congress.

Samizdat   An underground publication produced by dissidents.

Satellite states   Countries that are technically independent, which are nonetheless dominated politically and economically by another state.

Social malaise   A situation in which there are widespread social problems, as well as wide spread cynicism, despair and anxiety.

Socialism   An ideology and a political system based on the belief that people should be treated equally. Communists also use the term to refer to a historical period that occurs after capitalism but before Communism.

Soviets   Small, democratically elected councils, which emerged spontaneously after the February Revolution.

Sovnarkom   An economy in which the state and private enterprise both play a significant role.

Supranational   An organisation that has influence over several states.

Supreme Soviet   The organisation that made laws in the Soviet Union. Until Gorbachev's reforms it had very little power.

Tax in kind   A tax in which producers pay the government a proportion of what they make, rather than paying in money.

Tsar   The Russian Emperor and head of the Russian state, until his overthrow in 1917.

Vesenkha   The organisation that controlled the economy during War Communism.

Vozhd   A term meaning leader.

War Communism   A policy designed by the Communists to win the Russian Civil War through strict economic, political and military centralisation.

Key figures

Yuri Andropov (1914–84) Andropov was promoted within the Communist Party during the 1930s and became Soviet ambassador to Hungary in the mid-1950s. In 1967 he was appointed head of the KGB and used his influence in government to advocate suppression of dissidents and any anti-Soviet activity. He was promoted to the Politburo in 1973.

Lavrentiy Beria (1899–1953) Beria joined the Communist Party in 1917. He organised Stalin's purges of the Georgian Communist Party in the mid-1930s, and became head of the NKVD in 1938. Beria was one of Stalin's most trusted allies in government. During the Second World War he organised mass deportations and mass executions. His execution in 1953 marked the end of the use of mass terror as a political weapon in the Soviet Union.

Leonid Brezhnev (1906–81) Born in Ukraine, Brezhnev joined the Party in 1929. During the Great Terror he received a series of promotions as his superiors were purged. In 1952 Stalin promoted him to the Politburo. From 1962 he became increasingly critical of Khrushchev and was central to the plot to remove him from mid-1964. He suffered a heart attack in 1975 and was in poor health for the rest of his life.

Nikolai Bukharin (1888–1938) A committed Communist, Bukharin was one of the youngest Party members to play a key role in Lenin's government. From 1925 to early 1928 Bukharin was the most prominent figure in Soviet government. He was respected as a sincere and trustworthy Communist. In 1925 he formed an alliance with Stalin, known as the Duumvirate. Bukharin was executed during Stalin's Great Purge.

Konstantin Chernenko (1911–85) Born into a working-class family, Chernenko joined Komsomol in 1929 and the Party in 1931. He became friends with Brezhnev in the late 1940s and gained high office following Khrushchev's fall. He was one of the front-runners to replace Brezhnev on his death in 1982. Despite being extremely ill, he became leader of the Soviet Union in 1984.

Mikhail Gorbachev (1931–) Gorbachev was the last leader of the Soviet Union. His goal was to reform Communism in order to make it more successful. Gorbachev played a key role in ending the Cold War, in causing the break-up of the Eastern Bloc and in the collapse of the USSR.

Nikita Khrushchev (1894–1971) Worked as a miner in Ukraine, joining the Communists in 1918. He was elected to the Central Committee in 1934 and became leader of the Communist Party in Ukraine in 1935. His poor background made him popular with ordinary Russians. He was responsible for partial de-Stalinisation of the Soviet Union. He was removed from power in 1964. Khrushchev remained committed to Soviet socialism, believing it to be a superior system to capitalism and democracy until his death in 1971.

Sergei Kirov (1886–1934) Born into a poor family, Kirov became a leading member of the Communist Party in the 1920s. He was a Stalinist, who supported collectivisation, the Five-Year Plans and the use of political terror. Stalin viewed him as a potential rival.

Vladimir Lenin (1870–1924) A Marxist, revolutionary, journalist and intellectual, Lenin became leader of the Bolsheviks after a split in the Social Democratic Party in 1903. He led the Communists to seize power in 1917, and led them to victory in the Civil War. Successive Soviet leaders looked back to Lenin for their inspiration.

Vyacheslav Molotov (1890–1986) A committed member of the Communist Party, Molotov supported Stalin's key policies in the late 1920s and 1930s and played a central role in the Soviet government from 1930 to 1956. He was committed to Stalinist policies, and was critical of reforms under Khrushchev.

Joseph Stalin (1878–1953) Born into a poor Georgian family, Stalin was educated in a Church school. Stalin joined the Bolsheviks in 1903. Stalin was forced into exile by the Tsar's secret police due to his revolutionary activity. Stalin was a member of Lenin's first Politburo and played a major role in government under Lenin, before becoming leader of the Soviet Union after Lenin's death.

Leon Trotsky (1879–1940) A Marxist, revolutionary, journalist and intellectual, Trotsky came to fame as revolutionary leader of the St Petersburg Soviet in 1905. For many years, he was engaged in public disputes with Lenin. However, he joined the Communists in 1917 and played a leading role in Lenin's government. His heroic reputation was enhanced by his leadership of the Red Army during the Civil War. Trotsky was forced out of the Communist Party in 1928, and went into exile. He was assassinated by one of Stalin's agents in 1940.

Boris Yeltsin (1931–2007) Yeltsin was the first President of the Russian Federation after the fall of the Soviet Union. He joined the Communist Party in the early 1960s. From 1985 to 1987 Yeltsin was a keen supporter of Gorbachev's reforms. Yeltsin resigned from the Politburo in 1987 in protest at the slow pace of reform. He played a key role in the destruction of the Soviet Union by using his power to advance radical political and economic reform.

Grigory Zinoviev (1883–1936) A committed Communist, Zinoviev was Lenin's closest friend in the period 1902 to 1917. Zinoviev emerged as the front-runner to lead the Soviet Union in 1923. Between 1923 and 1925 he led the Triumvirate, an alliance of himself, Kamenev and Stalin, which effectively ruled the Soviet Union. Zinoviev was executed as a result of Stalin's first show trial in 1936.

Timeline

1914   Russia enters the First World War

1917   February   The February Revolution overthrows the Tsar

        March   A Provisional Government is established

        October   The October Revolution overthrows the Provisional Government

        Lenin establishes Sovnarkom

        Cheka established

1918   Lenin disbands Constituent Assembly

        Beginning of the Russian Civil War

        Lenin introduces state capitalism and War Communism

        Komsomol founded

1919   *Zhenotdel* created

1920   Department of Agitation Propaganda (Agitprop) set up

1921   End of the Russian Civil War

        Opposition political parties banned – Russia becomes a one-party state

        Lenin introduces the New Economic Policy (NEP)

        March Party Congress bans factions

1922   Glavlit, a new organisation, which oversaw a more systematic censorship regime, introduced

        Establishment of the Soviet Union

1923   The Soviet economy experiences the 'scissors crisis'

1924   January Lenin dies

1928   Stalin emerges as leader of Russia

        Stalin introduces the first Five-Year Plan

1929   Stalin orders compulsory collectivisation of Soviet farms

1932   Beginning of the Great Famine

1934   Kirov is murdered in Leningrad

        Yagoda appointed head of the NKVD

1935   The Great Terror begins with a purge of the Leningrad Communist Party

1936   Stalin removes high-profile opponents in the first Moscow Show Trials

        Yezhov becomes head of the secret police. The Great Terror intensifies

1941   German invasion leads to Soviet entry into the Second World War

1945   Second World War ends

1947   Vaccines for common diseases such as typhus and malaria made universally available

1953   Stalin dies

        Khrushchev launches the Virgin Lands Scheme

1955   Abortion legalised

1956   Khrushchev's Secret Speech – beginning of widespread de-Stalinisation

1957   Greater freedom of expression is permitted following the World Festival of Youth and Students

1964   Khrushchev removed from office. Brehznev begins to reverse Khrushchev's reforms

1966   New criminal code tightens laws on political dissents

        Sinyavsky–Daniel trial

1967   Andropov promoted to head of the KGB

1975   Brezhnev becomes increasingly ill and unable to govern effectively

1982   Brezhnev dies; Andropov initiates reforms to tackle corruption

1984   Andropov dies and is replaced by Chernenko before his reforms take effect

1985–86   Gorbachev introduces *uskorenie* – initial economic reforms

1986   The Twenty-Seventh Party Congress sets out a new programme for the Communist Party

1987–1990   Gorbachev initiates reforms intended to introduce market forces into the Soviet economy and political reforms to build support for greater economic change

1989   Communism falls across Eastern Europe

1990   Gorbachev appointed President of the Soviet Union

        Perestroika: Gorbachev begins to abandon fundamental aspects of the system such as single-party rule and command economy

1991   Coup to overthrow Gorbachev

        Yeltsin suspends the Communist Party in Russia

        Gorbachev resigns as President

        The Soviet Union ceases to exist

Mark scheme

A01 mark scheme

- **Analytical focus**
- **Accurate detail**
- **Supported judgement**
- Argument and structure

AS		A Level
1–4	Level 1 • **Simplistic, limited focus** • **Limited detail, limited accuracy** • **No judgement or asserted judgement** • Limited organisation, no argument	1–3
5–10	Level 2 • **Descriptive, implicit focus** • **Limited detail, mostly accurate** • **Judgement with limited support** • Basic organisation, limited argument	4–7
11–16	Level 3 • **Some analysis, clear focus (maybe descriptive in places)** • **Some detail, mostly accurate** • **Judgement with some support, based on implicit criteria** • Some organisation, the argument is broadly clear	
17–20	Level 4 • **Clear analysis, clear focus (maybe uneven)** • **Sufficient detail, mostly accurate** • **Judgement with some support, based on valid criteria** • Generally well organised, logical argument (may lack precision)	13–16
	Level 5 • **Sustained analysis, clear focus** • **Sufficient accurate detail, fully answers the question** • **Judgement with full support, based on valid criteria (considers relative significance)** • Well-organised, logical argument communicated with precision	17–20

AO3 mark scheme

- Interpretation and analysis of the extracts
- Knowledge of issues related to the debate
- Evaluation of the interpretations

AS		A Level
1–4	**Level 1** • **Limited level comprehension of the extracts demonstrated through selecting material** • **Some relevant knowledge, with limited links to the extracts** • Judgement has little or no support	1–3
5–10	**Level 2** • **Some understanding of the extracts demonstrated by describing some of their relevant points** • **Relevant knowledge added to expand on details in the extracts** • Judgement relates to the general issue rather than the specific view in the question. It has limited support	4–7
11–16	**Level 3** • **Understanding of the extracts demonstrated through selecting and explaining some of their key points** • **Relevant knowledge of the debate links to or expands some of the views given in the extracts** • Judgement relates to some key points made by the extracts. It has some support	8–12
17–20	**Level 4** • **Understanding of the extracts demonstrated through analysis of their interpretations, and a comparison of the extracts** • **Relevant knowledge of the debate integrated with issues raised by the extracts. Most of the relevant aspects of the debate are discussed – although some may lack depth** • Judgement relates to the interpretations of the extracts and is supported by a discussion of the evidence and interpretations of the extracts	13–16
	Level 5 • **Interpretation of the extracts demonstrated through a confident and discriminating analysis of their interpretations, clearly understanding the basis of both their arguments** • **Relevant knowledge of the debate integrated in a discussion of the evidence and arguments presented by the extracts** • Judgement relates to the interpretations of the extracts and is supported by a sustained evaluative argument regarding the evidence and interpretations of the extracts	17–20

Answers

1: Communist government in the USSR, 1917–85.

Page 5, Spot the mistake

The paragraph doesn't focus on the question.

Page 7, Identify the concept

How accurate is it to say that there were major changes in the role of the Communist Party in the years 1918–28? *change/continuity*

Was Lenin's ideology the main reason for the creation of a one-party state in the USSR in the years 1918–28? Explain your answer. *cause* **AS**

To what extent was Lenin responsible for the growing centralisation of Communist government in the years 1918–28? *cause*

Was the creation of a one-party state the main consequence of Communist government in the years 1918–28? Explain your answer. *consequence* **AS**

How far do you agree that the Civil War was the most significant factor in the centralisation of Communist power in the years 1918–28? *significance*

Page 7, Identify key terms

How accurate is it to say that there were <u>major changes</u> in <u>the role of the Communist Party</u> in the years 1918–28?

To what extent was <u>Lenin responsible</u> for the <u>growing centralisation</u> of Communist government in the years 1918–28?

Page 11, Eliminate irrelevance

One of the essential features of Communist government that changed dramatically between 1921 and 1953 was the power of the Communist Party. ~~The Communist Party seized power in 1917 as a result of the October Revolution.~~ By 1921 the Communist Party controlled the government. While Party rule was centralised and authoritarian, there was still debate within the Communist Party. Indeed, even after the ban on factions, debate continued over key issues such as economic policy. This changed significantly under Stalin. During Stalin's rise to power Stalin criticised his opponents for not being true Leninists. ~~All Communists were influenced by the thought of the German philosopher Karl Marx.~~ During the 1930s Stalin's terror attacked Communists with different views. This changed the nature of the Party significantly, by establishing a new ideological orthodoxy, which effectively ending freedom of debate in the Communist Party.

Page 13, Identify an argument

The first conclusion contains the argument.

2: Industrial and agricultural change, 1917–85

Page 19, Spot the mistake

The paragraph is focused and contains some accurate and relevant detail, but it does not conclude with an analytical link back to the question.

Page 27, Eliminate irrelevance

As well as promoting economic development, ~~government economic policies also played a role in promoting political stability. Lenin's Decree on Land won over the support of the peasants, which was crucial in the early phases of the revolution. Similarly, the NEP won back the support of the peasants in 1921.~~ However, Communist economic policy was not wholly successful at promoting political stability. By 1921 War Communism had ruined farming to such an extent that there was famine and revolt in Tambov and Kronstadt. Similarly, Collectivisation led to revolt in the countryside. ~~Rebellion against the government was particularly strong in Ukraine.~~ Worse still, a government-created famine between 1932 and 1933 resulted in 5 million deaths. ~~Stalin's industrial policy also created problems, for example the failure to invest in light industry meant that consumer goods were constantly in short supply. Moreover, Stalin did very little to help the 25 million people who were homeless following the war.~~ Therefore, economic development only partially created political stability as the economy under Stalin never really addressed the needs of the people.

Page 27, Identify the concept

How far do you agree that the introduction of the NEP in 1921 was the main turning point in Communist economic policy in the years 1917–53? *change/continuity*

How successful was Communist economic policy in the years 1917–53? *consequence* **AS**

To what extent did the aims of the Communist economic policy change in the years 1917–53? *change/continuity*

How accurate is it to say that Stalin's policies thoroughly modernised the Soviet economy in the years 1928–53? *consequence*

Was the failure of the NEP the main reason for Stalin's economic reforms of 1928–29? Explain your answer. *cause* **AS**

Page 31, Eliminate irrelevance

In some areas, such as consumer goods, the living standards of Soviet citizens improved dramatically in the years 1945–64. ~~Between 1928 and 1941 living standards had been low because of Stalin's Five-Year Plans, which included very few resources for creating consumer goods. This period was worse than the period under the NEP in which food tended to be plentiful.~~ In 1945, after the Second World War, consumer goods were scarce. ~~Stalin wanted to rebuild the Soviet Union's industrial economy, so consumer goods were not a priority. Also, Stalin wanted to re-arm because of the growing Cold War.~~ However, after 1953 the government attempted to improve living standards. Khrushchev's Seven-Year Plan made consumer goods a priority and his Corn Campaign emphasised the need to produce more food. Neither was wholly successful, but the availability of consumer goods did improve, which meant that there was some improvement in living standards between 1945 and 64.

3: Control of the people, 1917–85

Page 39, Eliminate irrelevance

There was extensive government control over the religious aspects of people's lives in the years 1918-53. ~~Lenin argued that religion was an enemy of freedom. He also believed that people who respected the teaching to the Church would never fully embrace Communist ideology.~~ Government control over religion was extended through terror. From 1918-53 terror was used extensively against the Orthodox Church. For example, Orthodox Priests in Moscow were massacred in January 1918 following a Church decree excommunicating the

Bolsheviks. ~~Stalin introduced big changes in policy such as the Five-Year Plans.~~ But he continued to attack religious groups. For example, during collectivisation many Church buildings were closed and turned into grain stores. What is more, he destroyed Islamic groups such as Sufi groups in Turkestan. Nonetheless, not all religious activity was tightly controlled. Lenin's government funded Islamic schools, and Muslims were encouraged to join the Party during the 1920s. Similarly, Stalin ended censorship of Church magazines, and allow some churches to re-open. Therefore, religion was tightly controlled, but control of religion was not complete because of the compromises made by the regime.

Page 45, Identify key terms

How accurate is it to say that Communist policy towards the arts <u>became increasingly repressive</u> in the years 1918–53?

How far do you agree that Soviet culture was <u>transformed</u> in the years 1918–53?

Page 45, You're the examiner

Level 4 as it is clearly focused on the right topic, concept and period, it deploys sufficient accurate and relevant detail, and it concludes with an analytical link back to the question.

Page 47, Identify the concept

To what extent were the cultural developments of the 1920s suppressed by Stalin's regime? *similarity/difference or change/continuity*

How far did government policy towards arts and culture change in the years 1953–85? *change/continuity* **AS**

To what extent did the Soviet secret police deal successfully with opposition in the years 1918–53? *consequence* **AS**

To what extent did the fundamental features of Stalin's government remain in place in the period 1953–85? *change/continuity*

How successful were government cultural policies in promoting political stability in the USSR in the years 1928–64? *consequence*

Page 47, You're the examiner

The answer shows Level 4 characteristics as it is clearly focused on the question, deploys accurate and relevant detail and presents a supported evaluation of the extent of change.

4: Social developments, 1917–85

Page 51, Spot the mistake

This paragraph does not contain sufficient accurate and relevant detail to achieve a mark in Level 4.

Page 55, Identify key terms

How far do you agree that in the years 1918–53 Soviet women made <u>substantial gains</u> in their <u>position</u> and <u>status</u>?

How accurate is it to say that women in the Soviet Union experienced only <u>limited changes</u> in their employment opportunities in the years 1953–85?

Page 57, Eliminate irrelevance

Divorce was one area where there were major changes in Communist family policy. ~~In the early years Alexandra Kollontai advocated free love and introduced experiments in communal living.~~ Lenin was also critical of traditional marriage and therefore he introduced easily accessible divorce. This changed radically under Stalin. During the 'Great Retreat' of the 1930s divorce was made much more difficult. Divorce became an expensive process, costing at least one week's wages. Moreover, divorced fathers were required to pay at least one-third of their income to their former wives to support their children. ~~Stalin also banned contraception, although there were more employment opportunities for women under the Five-Year Plans.~~ New divorce laws introduced in 1965 made divorce easier to obtain. Consequently, by 1979 around a third of marriages ended in divorce. Therefore, Soviet divorce policy changed significantly because there were reforms in the 1930s and again in the 1960s which changed government policy towards divorce dramatically.

Page 57, Identify an argument

The second conclusion contains the argument.

Page 59, You're the examiner

This paragraph has the characteristics of Level 4 as it is focused clearly on the question, contains sufficient detail to support its point and concludes with an analytical link back to the question.

Page 61, Identify the concept

How far do you agree that Soviet family life was transformed in the years 1918–64? *change/continuity*

How successful were Soviet educational policies in the years 1953–85? *consequence*

To what extent were there changes in Soviet social policy in the years 1918–64? **AS** *change/continuity*

Were Khrushchev's economic reforms the main reason for the decline in the Soviet economy in the years 1953-85? Explain your answer. **AS** *cause*

How accurate is it to say that there was very little difference in the social and economic policies of Communist governments under Khrushchev and Brezhnev? *similarity/difference*

5: What explains the fall of the USSR, c.1986–91

Page 71, Write the question

In the light of differing interpretations, how convincing do you find the view that 'Gorbachev's botched attempt to reform the political system' (Extract 1) led to the collapse of the Soviet Union?

How far do you agree with the view that Gorbachev's political reforms led to the collapse of the Soviet Union? **AS**

Page 85, Write the question

In the light of differing interpretations, how convincing do you find the view that the break-up of the Soviet Union was due to 'the new freedom and political pluralism' introduced in the later 1980s? (Extract 1)

How far do you agree with the view that the Soviet Union collapsed due to Gorbachev's political reforms? **AS**